THE THI

THE
THEBAN
ORACLE

DISCOVER THE MAGIC OF THE
ANCIENT ALPHABET THAT
CHANGES LIVES

GREG JENKINS, PH.D.

San Francisco, CA / Newburyport, MA

First published in 2014 by Weiser Books
Red Wheel/Weiser, LLC
With offices at:
665 Third Street, Suite 400
San Francisco, CA 94107
www.redwheelweiser.com

ISBN: 978-1-57863-549-8

Library of Congress Cataloging-in-Publication Data available upon request.
Cover design by Jim Warner
Interior by Kathryn Sky-Peck
Typeset in Centaur

MA
Printed in Canada
10 9 8 7 6 5 4 3 2 1

CONTENTS

Chapter Four

R: *Interference, Disturbance, Submission, Withdrawal*

S: *Wealth, a Tribute, a Spiritual Path, the Unseen*

T: *Tranquility, Simplicity, Joy*

U, V, W: *The True Male Significance, Divine Silence, Emotional Transition*

X: *Darkness and Light, Coexisting Differences, Misconception, Judgment*

Y: *Cherubic Protection, Security, Divine Mortality*

Z: *A Portal or Entrance, an Elevated Transposition*

Ending Stone: *Ending to a Life Process, Life Transition, Concurrence*

Mystery Stone: *An Unknowable Path, the Mystery of*
    Arcane Origins, Spiritual Freedom

Chapter Five

Chapter Six

> *Theban Spell for Finding True Love*
> *Theban Spell to Restore Lost Love*

> *Theban Negativity Cleansing Incense Ritual*
> *Theban Negativity Releasing Ritual*

Chapter Seven

This book and the wonders of the Theban mysteries
are fondly dedicated to:

Jami Vass and Leslie Anne McFadyen,
who listened with care and love, and who offered me their
admiration and understanding during dark times.

Also to Isabelle Moller,
who first introduced me to the many philosophical ideals
of a new age of positive thinking,

and to William Bryant Garrick,
a most worthy acolyte . . . These warm regards in return.

I offer this creation to my father, Gordon Clinton Jenkins,
who left us far too soon. You were the most noble and honest man I have ever
known . . . You will always be missed.

NOTE TO THE READER

The majesty and wonder of the Theban enigma and its significance to the realms of ancient magick has been and continues
to be of great inspiration for modern scholars. Past the initial formulation and construction of this codex and oracle system devised
centuries ago, right on through its modern applications, I found
an incredible ease associated with recognizing and indeed compre-
hending its seemingly mystical placement beyond the typical understanding since its origin. Whether engaged in the task of scholarly
research, or while in the practice and testing of this codex system as
a tool for oraclelike practices, I discovered a systematic and remarkable flow of wisdom appearing to me in an auspicious comport-
ment. Indeed, I have no doubt that the beholder of this system,
whether used as a game with friends and family, or as an oracle that
has survived the centuries, will also find a singular magick, which
emanates from this unique means of divination, serving you well
throughout the years to come.

Although at first glance the contents of this book may appear
to be highly intense in comprehension, requiring many skills within
the area of both low and high magick, it is designed specifically
for both those who possess an average understanding of the magi

arts, and those who already embrace a higher awareness in such pre-ternatural realms. In either case, I am sure you will find a particular feeling of enlightenment and a sense of the sacred within the worlds of the Medieval metaphysics and the Theban Oracle, both as a game of wisdom and as a method of personal transformation.

I feel it important to explain that this oracle's primary functions are to aid the user in the gentle art of living through one's own spiritual intuitions. The stones you will hold in your hands will absorb, assess, and spiritually relate what is already within you. Your spirit and the incredibly intense and interlaced patterns of your psyche will pass on to these stones. In essence, they will convey your personal and sacred vibrations via a form of psychic osmosis. The answers you receive, though seemingly esoteric at times, will resonate with that which is already within you . . . for you are the one holding the force of the universe in your hands.

The process of the Theban Oracle was designed to enhance the deeply rooted psychic awareness we all possess within us. While for some the process of psychic catharsis will come naturally, there will be those who will need to delve deeper into their soul before a true understanding can take place. Have the patience and tenacity to keep practicing, and an awareness of the divine will become more pronounced for you, as it has for me. In the end, you will find clarity in even the most arcane aspects of your life and find the solutions to many of the problems you face each and every day.

Many of us who are involved in the sacred arts of magick and divination understand that these natural gifts of divine presence and heavenly assistance are ever present within us as individual beings, as well as surrounding us as a whole family; therefore, it is vital that we take the next soulful steps in improving our state of mind, emotions, and spirit. Because we understand that the love and compassion within each of us at times may falter and wane from the stresses we encounter daily, I implore all who take part in this experience to find your sacred place beyond the often soulfully sick world in which we live.

Before using the Theban stones, find a sacred place that relates only to you in which to become calm and spiritually centered. Whether this may be in your home or another place of quiet contemplation, focus on looking beyond the madness that coexists in our world today, and offer yourself the freedom to find your spiritual bearings. Only by pursuing and practicing this affirmation and action will you find the answers and heavenly awareness you so richly desire—and deserve.

With this wish and blessing, I invite you to take this spiritual journey in safety and enjoyment. May the heavens illuminate its wisdom for you as it has done for me, and may you find your destiny within this oracle, designed for the enigmatic realities of woman and man, and discover the gentle wisdom of our celestial Mother and Father.

ℙℤℐℳℐℤ ⅋ℤ ⱵℲ∪ℤⱵ ℅ℳℲ

ACKNOWLEDGMENTS

This book, its research, and the indescribable findings—which have been revealed to me throughout my journey—are devoted to those who have the strength and commitment to travel beyond the confines of accepted thought, and who have endured the often dark and foreboding realities of all their incarnations, especially for those who lost their lives in the name of free thought, and for the healing of others in the name of all that's right and good.

I wish to acknowledge and pay reverence to the late Rev. Dr. Brian Glenn Turkington, Ph.D. Though a truly devout gentleman, a grounded psychotherapist, and a scholar in all things pertaining to religion, metaphysics, and psychology, he never judged others in the name of his faith or his God; instead he listened and healed those under his care. I thank you for your mentorship and gracefulness. I also wish to acknowledge both Dr. Sedgwick Grange, D.Sc., anthropologist, sociologist, and folklorist, and Fr. Lionel Fanthorpe, one of England's most notable sages and faithful men. Both have afforded great wisdom on a moment's notice to assist all in the many aspects of the Medieval world and modern metaphysics and have entrusted me with the most sacred and revered of ancient texts from their private collections.

I also wish to thank Alison Bailey, curator, coordinator, and interpreter of early printed collections, and the staff at the British Library for their assistance and support during my research and for the use of their most venerated and time-honored collections. Thanks as well to Mr. Joseph H. Peterson and The Twilit Grotto: Archives of Western Esoterica, likely the most comprehensive collection of historically accurate documents on metaphysics and the occult today. And finally, I wish to pay my respects to the enigmatic and historically elusive woman named "Bethany," who to this day remains a mystery to New England's luminaries and occult scholars. For the ancient wisdom and rituals you took part in, and for unknowingly opening my eyes to a much larger world of understanding, I offer my thanks.

Chapter One

THE OCCULT ARTS AND SCIENCES: AN INTRODUCTION TO MEDIEVAL METAPHYSICS

Before we begin with the science and methodology of the Theban alphabet as it applies to the ancient divinatory arts, it is important to briefly discuss the concepts of magick and its practical interpretations in history. In order to achieve any success, we must first lay to rest the many misconceptions regarding magick and the occult, which may have altered our perceptions and beliefs. Second, we must also put to rest the incorrect concept that all who partake in the occult arts are of an evil mindset or plan for the destruction or misfortune of others. This childish notion is simply not true.

Finally, in order to find any rhyme or reason for those things that incorporate the concept of magick, we must completely eliminate the negative aspects in our thinking habits. In fact, we must open our senses to the possibility of such things, that all that we do is done for the benefit of all, beyond the common selfishness that has invaded the psyches of so many today. By realizing this simple idea, we will cease all self-devised ignorance and take meaningful steps into a larger universe. If hatred and revenge reside in the mind, such attributes will be incorporated into any magickal work. Therefore, we must be mindful of our feelings and our intent when involved in such work, so that we harm none during our journeys. Keeping this in mind, you are now ready to begin your sacred quest.

It may be assumed that the basic concept of modern magick and the belief in the powers of the unseen world and nature have been realized in one form or another since the dawn of time. Humanity's probing into the universe, within our own immediate environment as well as into the unknown, led to the comprehension of psychic divination, which may have been cultivated or fine-tuned during the early Middle Ages. Today, however, when we think of magick as something tangible, we might first think of the quintessential magician who performs tricks and sleight-of-hand illusions for the sake of entertainment. Indeed, although we may be completely mesmerized by these phenomenal feats of skill and illusion, this art form has unintentionally bastardized the true concept of what we call magick.

If we look to the Hollywood ideal of the supernatural aspects of magick, we may see a bountiful selection of wizards and similar magi either fighting to save the world or working desperately to destroy it. With images from J. R. R. Tolkien's *Lord of the Rings*, and the wise wizard Gandalf battling his evil nemesis the wizard Saruman, we can see the almost endless battle between the forces of good and evil. Within the context of J. K. Rowling's fantastic world of Harry Potter and Hogwart's School of Witchcraft and Wizardry, the escapades of the fledgling wizards and witches are certainly delightful, albeit a rather one-sided and childlike representation of magick and the "old religion." Although entertaining, such films and novels actually end up doing irreparable damage to the true nature of the magickal arts.

When we search our collective memories regarding true magick as a supernatural force, we may conjure up visions of King Arthur, his wonderful kingdom of Avalon, and the mystical magus known as Merlin. Although this wise wizard, who is represented in most accepted versions of the Arthur legend, is at least somewhat true, the actual nature and works of the man himself have far too often been fabricated in order to entice and impress, rather than support the actual facts. In truth, the wizard Merlin (c. 440–540), the mystical Druid traditionally known as Myrddin, Merlyn, Emrys, or Ambrosias to historians and practitioners of the old faiths, remains the archetypal icon of magick in Western civilization. This 6th-century Welsh magus was one of many Druids who practiced and instructed the divinatory arts. By aligning his research to the understanding of all things related to the elementals, he found that all things on the earth held within them a source of power and sentience, which would produce a bond with those who are sensitive to it, thus creating a unique union between man and nature. By acknowledging these supernatural forces and the realities of Water,

Air, Earth, and Fire, as well as all living creatures, Merlin gleaned a profound understanding of the most numinous secrets that existed within all of nature, which he simply referred to as the essence, spiritual manna that exists on earth and throughout the universe.

According to traditional legends, Merlin was able to communicate with nature as a living, breathing element of life, believing that the earth was indeed a living creature that must be respected and obeyed in full, in order for man to live in harmony with his environment. Though man had and continues to have many problems grasping this simple edict, Merlin understood this concept with complete clarity. Simply stated, in order to continue his bond with nature, man must look deeply within nature itself, which means that all living things, as well as the herbs and roots, the rivers and oceans, and even the minerals of the earth, must be unconditionally respected and appreciated. In the end, Merlin was able to take the wisdom of nature and instruct those who were willing to listen and learn.

Although the true man known as Merlin and his teachings are the accumulation of many oral traditions, which have no doubt been altered over the many centuries, they incorporate a hint of truth and set forth a foundation for eternal knowledge nonetheless. Even when immersed in the romantic ether of the Arthurian legends, in whichever manner this enigmatic wizard is portrayed, we may look upon his image as a foundation of the metaphysical arts and sciences, where nature itself is the primary source of all goodly works. As time progressed, the teachings of Merlin would remain almost exclusively within pan-Celtic cultures, seemingly fading during the reign of the Roman Empire, until a resurgence of public interest after Rome was overthrown by the warlord Odoacer and his Germanic invaders around 476 AD. In later centuries the purveyors of high magick, such as Honorius of Thebes, would incorporate many magickal sigils and characters—to be aligned with the various angels, daemons, and other creatures of the natural and supernatural worlds—into their magickal works. Honorius of Thebes is said to have taught many select students in the magickal arts, and to some extent had even unified the Catholic Church with several magi traditions. What is more, documentation has supported that even Emperor Charlemagne and other notable rulers were instructed in the magickal arts, in order to protect themselves during times of war and plague, and of course, against sorcery by adversaries.

These holy men are believed to have used many ancient inscriptions, druidic prayers, and celestial seals and characters in order to aid in their success. Such "art magick," as it was called, though controversial for a ruler to indulge in, is nonetheless accounted to be factual by modern-day scholars. In fact, many popes, bishops, and archbishops were known to have participated in many forms of magick and spell craft. Religious wizards such as Popes Sylvester II, Leo III, and Urban V were all known to have employed the use of magickal talismans and seals, cryptic alphabets, and so-called divine letters for various purposes, while at the same time damning others to death for doing the same.

During this period other noteworthy sages and magi, such as Thomas Aquinas, Arnaud de Villeneuve, Roger Bacon, Petrus de Abano, and Johannes Trithemius, were leaving their marks within the realms of the occult arts and creating history by learning and teaching many protected secrets, while at the same time safeguarding their traditions from the witch hunts of the day. While such scholars were using magick talismans and characters; employing the Zodiac, celestial, and angelic alphabets for inscribing their written incantations; instructing others in the magickal traditions of the ancient Greeks, Babylonians, Egyptians, and Israelites; or experimenting in alchemical potions with zeal, it would not be long before the holy inquisitors would hear of such questionable practices and wage holy war against all surveyors of wisdom beyond the accepted biblical foundations of the day.

When the Italian scholar and physician Petrus de Abano authored his magnum opus, *Magical Elements,* new thinking commenced toward the schools of magick and its practice. Belonging to a secret group of French magi, his literature and teachings not only inspired his followers but eventually caught the eye of the mighty Church, thus triggering his unfortunate arrest and imprisonment, and eventual execution. Although his and other magickal texts were prominent in some circles, many would be lost to the madness of the many inquisitions that occurred during that time. And even though the surviving works of Petrus de Abano certainly helped in the clarification of many ancient teachings, much of his research, as well as notable literary manuscripts, were assigned to the annals of mystery and forever lost. By the early 15th century, the famous occult scholar Heinrich Cornelius Agrippa was able to collect the most arcane knowledge of history, thus constructing his now famous literary work, *De Occulta Philosophia*, or the *Three Books of Occult Philosophy*. Indeed, it was Agrippa who referred to the scholarly occult works of Petrus de Abano, Honorius of Thebes, and the Abbot Johannes Trithemius for their scholarly contributions. His friend and mentor Johannes Trithemius's famous work, the *Steganographia*, was to be the primary inspiration to his research and practice.

Most of the aforementioned literary works were either lost or fragmented and contained a few examples of Dr. John Dee's *Enochian Alphabet* and various cryptic angelic and celestial writings, such as *Malachim, Passing of the River,* and the most enigmatic script of all, known as *Honorian,* or *Theban*. The true nature and purpose of these alphabets were just as much a mystery then as they are today. Indeed, such works seemed to fade almost into complete obscurity, taking on a darker and even sinister image as time progressed.

During the Renaissance, these occult scholars represented a rebirth of ancient magick traditions, which they claimed to have been seminal to the Hebrew, Arabic, and Egyptian magickal foundations. Undeniably, the reinstitution of these most arcane metaphysical arts and sciences would reinvent and impel the spirit of the ancients into modern times. It was the French scholar, physician, and seer Michel

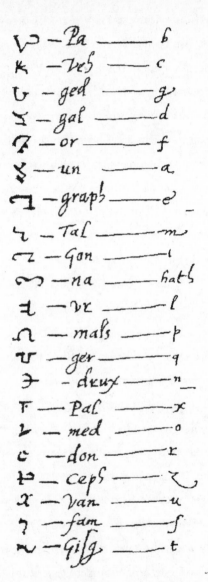

Dr. John Dee's Enochian alphabet of 1582

de Nostradame, known simply as Nostradamus, who is remembered for perfecting several ancient astrological traditions, and who inspired many of the modern meanings to the natural sciences, as well as instituting new thinking toward the occult sciences. Nostradamus worked closely with the writings of both Agrippa and Trithemius, being instructed in the arts and histories of clairvoyance and divination, which contributed to his foresight, and ultimately, to his famous works of prophecy known as the quatrains.

Dr. John Dee, the Royal Magus and advisor to Queen Elizabeth I of England, was also strongly influenced by the works of Agrippa and added many of his findings to his own works of Enochian magick and necromancy. Dee was so impressed with Agrippa's works that he would pass many of his ideas along to other scholars throughout the civilized world. One scholar in particular was Giordano Bruno, the famous Italian occultist and author of *De Magia*, who spoke highly of Agrippa's beliefs and concentrated on such topics, thus influencing new theoretical concepts and teachings for centuries to come.

Among the many traditions within the works of history's most diverse occult scholars, the topic of cryptic alphabets and cipher writing had not only intrigued but had also infuriated them. For as much information as they did indeed have of history's ancient secrets, nonetheless many aspects of the occult sciences and metaphysics had eluded them. Of these cryptic writings, the mystical Theban alphabet remained one of the most esoteric. Many Hebrew

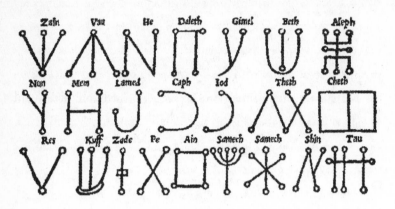

The writing called Malichim

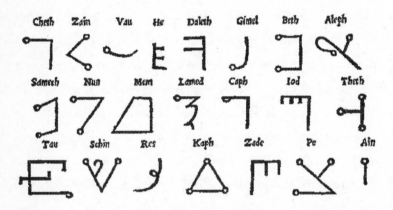

The writing called The Passing of the River

Examples of eye writing

scholars referred to the Theban alphabet as a form of "eye writing," so called because of its unique rounded edges and mysterious styling (see facing page). It was also referred to as angelic in nature, due to its later association with the inscription to angels and the hierarchy in the heavenly realms. The Theban script, although delightful to view, would remain a historical conundrum.

Even when falling into a veritable age of anonymity, some fragments of these ancient tomes and scrolls of sorcery had been assigned the dubious position of artifact, to be held as exhibits in many stately British and European museums and universities, to rest behind glass or buried deep within the stacks of ancient athenaeums. Indisputably, the mysteries of the secret ciphers and arcane scripts would appear dead to scholars and laymen alike. The magick of the once sought-after and often-to-be-feared books had seemed to lose its inscrutable luster, practical appeal, and supernatural charm. Either due to the numbing ages of conformity or the many advances of industry and technology, the essence of the written words of magick seemed to vanish forever.

By the 18th and 19th centuries, however, a fledgling spiritual movement brought about the age of the mystic once again and instituted a new era of spiritual inquiries, as well as a sincere desire for hidden knowledge. The rebirth of these concepts had occurred throughout Europe and America, and the yearning for séances, consortiums on alchemy, and high magick, as well as the arts of divination and foresight, had literally become a new religion. As many researchers, scholars, and laymen alike were delving into the magickal arts with full force, it was only a matter of time before these tenacious people would rediscover the magickal books of the Middle Ages. The once shunned and locked-away tomes of magickal repute were now finding fresh minds to entice and edify. Once again the wisdom of the ages was illuminating the faithful and the wise throughout the world.

Because so much research and literature had been lost throughout history, whether due to angry mobs and witch hunters, or to the general neglect of its regents, such cunning wisdom might very well have been lost forever. Recently, however, the works by Heinrich Cornelius Agrippa and his *Three Books of Occult Philosophy*, as well as his alleged *Fourth Book of Occult Philosophy*, have been revised, translated, and edited for modern-day usage. Indeed, such scholarly pursuits may offer to their readers the chance to delve deeper into the realms of the unknown from an educated foundation. Although such cryptic writing structures as the Theban alphabet and other mystical representations are well expressed and quoted within these tomes, the overall matter, however, still continues to reek with the air of the unknown. Yet, if we give of ourselves in earnest to what these arcane segments of magickal lore are, such as the Theban script and its true meanings, and allow ourselves to become open to these ancient mysteries, such deep teachings may finally become clear.

Though these mysteries will no doubt continue in spite of the knowledge we already have concerning these ancient scripts and cipher codes, we may learn from the reasoning that came about for using them in the first place. To that end, when we apply such true and noble concepts to our daily lives, with the intent to offset all hatred and any article of ill will, we may eventually succeed in all our honest and righteous endeavors and prosper as a result. For this reason I have created this method of oracle; not as a way for predicting the future or advising the player on what to do in her life, but instead offering the player a chance to consider the kinds of wisdom that the ancient magi or wizards may have used in their day. Such combines ancient wisdom to instruct and foster a spiritual form of thought, with just the right amount of personal invention. It is not meant to solve our problems for us, but to offer us the opportunity to find our own ways by eliminating the many negative issues we face in life, and to understand whatever we may encounter in the future without fear or loathing. With this said, prepare yourself to go deeper within, by opening your intuitions and insight to much broader depths of knowledge and soulful wisdom.

Either through the understanding of the ancients or simply with a desire to better ourselves and our situations, in order to transverse beyond our falsely lit world, we begin to understand and rely on this ancient knowledge, transcend to a higher plane of awareness and reflection, and finally prepare ourselves for the sacred journey ahead. It is with this sentiment that I offer this work and its gentle purpose. The rest is up to you.

Chapter Two

INTRODUCTION TO THE THEBAN ALPHABET AND ITS MYSTERIOUS HISTORY

Of magic[k] . . . Producing its wonderful effects, by uniting the virtues of things through the application of them one to the other, and to their inferior suitable subjects, joining and knitting them together thoroughly by the powers and virtues of the superior bodies.

CORNELIUS AGRIPPA, *THREE BOOKS OF OCCULT PHILOSOPHY*: BK. I, CHAP. 2

The *Theban Oracle* serves as a process for self-wisdom and deep contemplation, where in the traditional method ancient sooth-sayers may have painted arcane symbols on stones or carved them on shards of wood and animal bones to express such foretelling. The Theban example employs such a method, and also pays homage to history's most notable men and women who made a place for themselves in the realms of magick, alchemy, and the esoteric disciplines. This book is designed to offer the reader whether acolyte or scholar, a manner from which to spiritually grow and eventually pass on to their peers or pupils. It is designed to foster wisdom that already exists within you, though not to substitute for your faith. In short, this process is not designed to represent any kind of magick in and of itself, but rather offer the player a chance to work out their issues and problems by way of the ancient sages and magi.

This book should be viewed as a game for testing one's own wisdom and for figuring out one's own destiny from a historical perspective, much like the magi of old would have done. It is designed for the player to propose detailed questions and then to search through the answers for personal meanings that are uniquely relevant to the player. It is formulated to foster ideas giving direction to one's life. This is the oracle that already exists within you! With that said, remember the words of the 19th-century occult scholar C. G. Leland: "Questions asked without faith, are not questions at all . . . As without a true question, one cannot obtain true faith." What does this mean? Simply that the questions you ask must be of a heartfelt nature, with the sincerity of a deeply thought-out inquiry. Questions that will lead to logical answers are formulated from within those using this divinatory game system. They will ultimately find the answer they are seeking, so long as they ask with soulful tenacity. Asking questions without a defined purpose, however, will only delay the insight you are truly searching for. Therefore, you must be true to yourself in order to find true success.

Historically, each item within divinatory processes, such as the Tarot cards or rune stones, will have a profound symbol and meaning attached to it, where each card or stone will represent a symbol within a spiritual context. The Theban alphabet or codex system also has such symbols designated to represent human luminaries and angelic personas that best correspond to the subject matter represented. Each associated symbol is designed to give the player an insightful and meaningful reflection of their innermost personal queries, and will offer various aspects of advice and wisdom that only the one engaged in the process could truly understand. A system that operates as precisely as other oraclelike processes, the Theban Oracle will prove precise and spiritually enlightening. Remember, though in essence a game, this process will open new pathways to personal realities and spiritual endeavors for you, so long as you're emotionally still and remain open to the answers received.

The Theban alphabet, as we have known it throughout history, was exemplified and expounded upon by Honorius of Thebes during the Middle Ages. It was also noted by Cornelius Agrippa in the 15th century. It was during this period when attention to the Theban script was reborn and used as a form of lettering or as a secret ciphering tool by those who wished to escape the noose and fiery pits of the Inquisitions. The Theban alphabet became an important tool for those wanting to secretly communicate with each other and safeguard their lives. As time progressed and fear of execution waned, the Theban alphabet was used for less crucial purposes. From initiation rites in secret sects and for sending private messages within pagan covens, to being used for the inscription of magickal names, spell casting, or even for the inscribing of candles and books of shadows, these elegant, runelike symbols would find a place of legend within the realms of magick and the pagan crafts.

Though many practitioners of Wicca, Druidism, and those of similar mindsets have taken part in ceremonies that have applied the Theban alphabet, many have never fully understood the potential or meaning of these cryptic symbols. To be sure, while such ciphers may have been used to pass information and warning to persecuted women and men during the dark times of history, the burning times, or even to enhance the craft in ritual, the true history and purpose of the Theban alphabet continues to remain in question by most scholars today. What we do know, however, is what the famed master of the occult, the celestial interpreter, magician, and scholar, Heinrich Cornelius Agrippa had written of the Theban text, giving us at least some possible origins to its cloudy history.

Agrippa provided a version of the Theban alphabet, referring to Petrus de Abano, the famous Medieval physician and occult chronicler, as being a central source of information. He wrote: "Of this kind of character [Theban] therefore are those which Apponus (Petrus de Abano) notes; as delivered by Honorius of Thebes." This appears to offer at least some historical significance, though continuing to rest in an almost unattainable mist of controversy. Undeniably, this passage tends to illustrate that the Theban alphabet, also referred to as "Honorian," had originally been formulated and penned by the

The Theban alphabet

mysterious magus known as Honorius of Thebes, the author of the 13th-century tome of magick, *Liber Juratus*, known by other names such as the *Liber Iuratus Honorii* and *The Sworne Booke of Honorius*.

Having researched Petrus de Abano's occult works, Agrippa found that one of his books, *The Heptameron*, or *The Magic Element*, which represents seven sacred days of magick, had discussed in detail the seven rites for conjuring angelic forces, one for each day of the week. This appears to be based on several Solomonic texts, such as *The Hebrew Key of Solomon* and *The Book of Light*. In fact, some believe that Agrippa found a correlation between many forms of celestial writings, including that of the Theban alphabet, as possibly having its origins in far earlier periods predating the Middle Ages by centuries. Agrippa believed that the Theban alphabet may have been directly related to the teachings of the angels in ancient Hebrew cultures, which was given directly to early man in order to

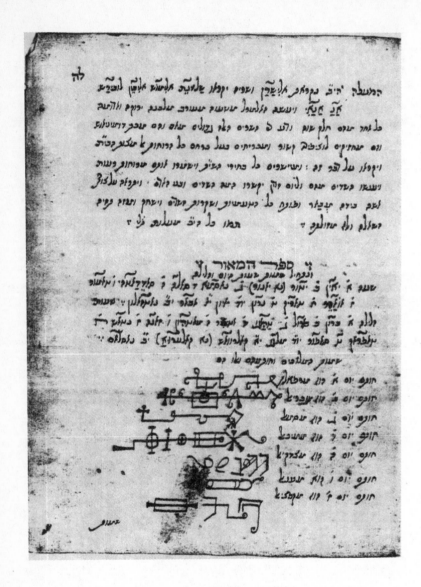

A page fom *The Heptameron*

defeat daemons, elementals, and the fallen caste of angel spawned by the Seraphim called the Nephilim. If true, this intriguing mystic script will afford itself the role of sanctity, far more than simply as a form of magick lettering.

The letters are common in Theban and in basic Latin, but the letters I and J count as one, as well as the letters U, V, and W, giving it twenty-four letters in all. In ancient Latin, the letters Y and Z did not appear until the 1st century BC. Therefore the Theban alphabet we see today had to have been created after the time of the Roman Empire, as it clearly has the Y and Z added. Though this simple fact does not explain the belief that this alphabet and similar ones predate the Romans by centuries, the possibility surely adds to the already mystical quality of the Theban alphabet, as we still cannot fathom what the original text must have looked like, or how Honorius of Thebes came to discover it, if in fact he did. In what appears to be a simple cipherlike code, and having no bearing in any known language, nor able to form the necessary elements to create verbiage as we might understand it, the alphabet has no other purpose other than to code common words. However, in the Hebrew alphabet, we can see a similar correlation, where certain letters will count as two or sometimes three. Although sentence structure for all flowing languages uses various systems in constructing consonants and vowels in order to make it comprehensible, the Theban example was used independently. It merely suffices as a method to deliberately confuse the reader from finding its intended meaning. We can, how-

Latin	Theban	Hebrew
a	૫	א
b	વ	ב
c	ખ	ג
d	ᶭ	ד
e	૨	ה
f	ᵞ	ו
g	ᶣ	ז
h	ᶣ	ח
i	ᶹ	ט
j	ᶹ	ט
k	ᶬ	י
l	૨	כ
m	ᶮ	ל
n	ᶵ	מ
o	ᶮ	
p	ᶮ	ס
q	૧	ע
r	ᶮ	פ
s	૪	צ
t	૪	ק
u	૮	ר
v	૮	ר
w	ᶮᶮ	ר
x	ᶮᵐ	ש
y	ᵚ	ת
z	ᶮᶣ	ז

ever, see in the table on the facing page how the Theban letters can be aligned with the Hebrew script.

Because the Theban alphabet remains a scholarly enigma, many have simply assigned this beautiful script to a conundrum of history, seeing it as a cryptic oddity with no true significance. Some feel that because it has a resemblance to the symbols of the Zodiac, it must have its basis therein. Yet still others feel that the works of the *Liber Juratus* and similar tomes offer enough proof of its intentions and reasoning, and assign Honorius of Thebes as the original innovator. Nonetheless, certain sects of magi have connected the particular codices of the Theban script to far earlier magical foundations, such as from the age of Adam, and in the pre-Hebrew works like the *Angelus Magnus Secreti Creatoris,* which was scripted in the long-dead language of "Chaldea." In either case, until a forthcoming archaeologist, anthropologist, theologian, or scholar of magick finds the truth about the Theban alphabet the most educated guesses must therefore make do.

Honorius of Thebes:
Secret Chronicler of the Ancients

The legend of Honorius of Thebes, according to many Medieval manuscripts and posthumous documents, suggest that in order to save the collected and time-honored works of high magick and ceremonial ritual from the tyrannical popes and cardinals of the day, a union of famed magi and wizards from Spain, Italy, Greece, and the rest of Europe, as well as from a mystical place known simply as Tholetus, banded together to collect, encode, and hide the sacred texts, tomes, and other fragments of historical magick works, in order to safeguard such wisdom of the ancients from the madness of the many inquisitions that were constantly arising.

History tells us that 811 masters hailing from Naples, Athens, and Toledo elected a man called Honorius, the son of Euclid, also known as the master of the Thebans, to cipher and encode the existing and ancient texts of magick. It is said that Honorius, along with the counsel of an angel called Hocroell, wrote seven volumes on the magickal arts. Out of these seven volumes, Honorius composed one book containing ninety-three chapters, in which is contained the truth and effects of magick and the ceremonial arts from at least two thousand years prior. This sworn book also contained the one hundred sacred names of God, thus transforming it into a most revered and sacred text, as well as making it a potentially dangerous item, should it fall into the wrong hands. Moreover, since angelic intervention delivered such wisdom, the enlightenment and spiritual illumination is evident in the information received by Honorius.

From the very moment this sacred book was devised and completed, no copy was to be delivered to anyone outside the fold of the magi. No copy of this sacred book was to be delivered to anyone unless he was a master magus or in danger of death. Because there were only a few original copies in existence, its legacy became known within only the highest of magickal orders. One of the highest rules for obtaining this sacred book was that the recipient should be a godly man of faith, which meant he had to be tested for at least one year by the aforementioned surviving council of magi. Moreover, *The Sworne Booke of Honorius* was to be reinstated to its master or his male descendants if death was imminent. If there was no male descendant to be found or any male deemed worthy enough to receive it, the book was ordered to be buried with its master, and was not to be given or passed down to any uncouth man, woman, or child. Indeed, these rules were so strict that even the most ardent of scholars of the magickal arts would suffer death rather than betray the confidence of Honorius and his council of magi. The disciples of Honorius swore never to reveal the secrets of this sacred tome to anyone, and in so doing, must keep every article of the oath that follows:

> In the name of Jesus Christ, our Lord and true and living God, I, Honorius, appoint in my book the work of Solomon; I profess that the divine mystery is the only arch-principle and that true invocation must come from the faith of the heart, which faith these works declare . . . Solomon said that there is only one God from whom all perfection and the effect of every work proceeds—SI. VM E. T A. V. V M

As generations passed, and many and varied works of magick arrived and departed in the process, some being lost forever, the

Theban script seemed to lie dormant through the passage of time until the early 19th century, when it would find public attention once again. An Englishman named Francis Barrett published an intriguing book in 1801 called *The Magus,* also known as *The Celestial Intelligencer.* Barrett, a student of history and chemistry and an avid researcher of metaphysics and occult philosophies, meticulously translated the Kabbalah and other ancient works into English. He also offered lessons in occult sciences and mysticism to anyone who wanted to learn. With his great enthusiasm for the metaphysical arts and sciences, it would be only a matter of time until he would discover the beautiful script that is the Theban alphabet.

For the most part, *The Magus* deals primarily with the natural forms of elemental magick, involving herbs, minerals, and magnetism, yet also details alchemy, numerology, talismanic, and ceremonial magick, as well as highlighting the use of the celestial scripts such as the Theban alphabet. Although *The Magus* was well received in many occult circles, it did not see as much popularity with the public until it was noticed by famed French magus Eliphas Levi, who crusaded to bring public interest to Barrett's work. After that, many practitioners and lay occultists alike were using the many magickal formats and rites of ritual from *The Magus,* thus inducting many people into the newly found spiritualist cliques. Barrett's work also attracted Montague Summers, the illustrious British historian, who not only supported Barrett's work in the professional realm but also aided him and others to usher in a fledgling era of enlightenment for the 19th and 20th centuries.

As time progressed, and many changes and advances in industry and technology came about, the age of spiritualism waned. Spiritual enchantments, the supernatural, and the creatures of the preternatural world retreated to the nether regions of man's imagination, becoming the objects of trick-or-treating and childish thinking rather than that of a science. Even though many considered such beliefs as witchcraft to exist outside the parameters of accepted religion, actually being evil in nature, the killing mobs would nonetheless lapse into the realms of history. The image of so-called wizards and witches would become a fantasy, as portrayed by popular literature of the day, rather than that of fact. The truth of the old religion seemed to drift away, becoming nothing more than a trick of the light or a huckster trying to gain your money. To be sure, the old religion seemed to have disappeared from everyday life, becoming nothing more than a mythology to the ignorant and naysayer alike.

As Western civilization entered the 20th century, many aspects of the occult philosophies would become dormant to most. Regardless, such beliefs would continue to be realized and practiced by a select few who still felt the calling for something different. The visions of these exclusive peoples continued to flourish in their hearts and minds, returning to the spiritual modalities of their ancient ancestors. In so doing, the need to research such past philosophies became clear, and it didn't take long for those select few to rediscover the mysteries that Honorius of Thebes and his contemporaries had created.

As research into the occult mysteries grew, and the free thinking movement began to rekindle its fires once again in the minds of scholar and layman alike, the works of Agrippa, Paracelsus, Michel de Nostradame, and many others would open new avenues for thought, offering spiritual answers to the most primal questions. Concepts like divination and the ceremonial arts began to blossom once again, and the ancient arts and sciences of the old religion would be reborn. Indeed, during the middle half of the 20th century, Gerald Brousseau Gardner, an anthropologist and collector of cultural antiquities, took a giant step toward the liberation of such free thinking and inspired the reintroduction of the old religion into modern society, both as a science and as a practice. Author of *High Magick's Aid* and *Witchcraft Today*, Gardner presented the ancient teachings in a new and enlightened manner, which prompted many to emulate him. Gardner moved away from the theatrics of those before him, ignored the false image magick and witchcraft was assigned by popular novels and films, and turned his back on the Satanic-like trappings of so-called modern witches. Instead, he offered an opposite alternative to the unfortunate Hollywood-like undertones the craft had incurred over the many years, and paved the way to new thinking toward the old religion. Gardner brought respectability to paganism and its practice, so much so that people were beginning to look upon such faiths in a far more favorable light than ever in the past. In the end, Gardner removed a good portion of the unrealistic darkness and sensationalism, and instilled a light of goodness and purpose toward those ancient practices, a concept that continues to this day.

In later years, Gardner would serve as curator for the Museum of Magic and Witchcraft on the Isle of Man, in the United Kingdom, and it was his profound interest in the old religion, particularly in ancient artifacts and mystical symbols, that reinstated the use of codex alphabets, including the Theban script, within modern applications. It was during Gardner's research on Agrippa's works, as well as on *The Sworne Booke of Honorius,* that he became interested in this beautiful yet alien script. Although it was still a mystery, he was able to use the Theban alphabet both as a way to write and as a representation of icons, animals, minerals, and natural powers such as a thunderstorm or to represent a season. Of course, this was not believed to be Gardner's idea alone, as many modern magi had speculated that it was Agrippa who aligned the hierarchy of certain angels as the source and heavenly purpose behind the Theban alphabet.

As years passed, some groups and open-minded individuals would assign various castes of angels and mystical creatures to coordinate with each of the twenty-four letters and the one ending mark, as well as assigning one "point" to signify an unknowable agent or purpose within the context of the magickal universe. This was intended to bestow respect to the unknowable thus fostering a sense of honor to the alphabet codex as a whole. Although the past reflections of an ancient magus and other aspects of the occult will always remain a mystery, we as practitioners and those of us who yearn for a greater understanding of ourselves and our universe may take certain liberties in order to secure our own personal methods in doing so. It was this concept that inspired *The Theban Oracle* as a device for personal foresight and soulful healing, as a subtle game steeped in morals, and for some, as a tool for personal divination.

As a researcher into the many aspects of the occult arts and sciences, as well as history, folklore, and oral traditions, I have become aware of many forms of divination, along with many of the so-called fortune-telling tools. Over the years, I have had the opportunity to work with many spiritual people from all walks of life and backgrounds. From university professors to voodoo celebrants and Wiccan high priestesses, to Native American shamans and modern-day soothsayers, I have noticed a profound interest in the divinatory arts. Thus began my quest into this intriguing aspect of the human condition, one of humankind's natural inclinations.

During my research, I began to see the power that many of the divinatory devices held for ancient peoples, not so much in producing any exact or definite answer, or to predict the future per se, but as an aid that would assist them in gazing deeply into their most profound queries with more reverence and compassion. I was able to look beyond the simple icons that the Tarot cards and rune stones offered, as well as the sometimes mysterious responses these divinatory tools might give in relation to one's inquiries. I found that if I reread the answer given, or perhaps took a few moments to digest that answer, I would discover a direct relation to my questions, thus creating a deeper understanding of the issues that lay before me, both the good and the bad.

In the context of being a tool for divination, *The Theban Oracle* is indeed designed as a game of wisdom and personal transformation. It is similar in many respects to popular divinatory tools used today; yet this system is devised to further produce insightful contemplation. Because those luminaries like Dr. John Dee, Cornelius Agrippa, Dr. Nicholas Flamel, and others assigned a caste of heavenly guardians to the Theban alphabet, there is an excitedly good feeling in them. Indeed, those who have partaken in this process during its research and formulation have agreed to this, saying that they felt something contenting about them, as what they learned about themselves was something perhaps divine in nature. Knowing not to entice or coerce, I simply explained the rules of the Theban divination process and offered the same meanings that you will find in this book. The results were both educational and enlightening, as I am certain you will also discover.

Ancient Wisdom of the Theban Oracle

Because there have been so few women and men able to look beyond the curtain of the mundane, risking life and limb in doing so, I have included such historical personalities with each of the Theban symbols in dedication to their devotion and sacrifice, which have culminated partly in the privilege of free thought that many cultures enjoy today. As a representation of their gift of hidden wisdom, each Theban symbol and luminary represented offers the use of these special stones as a unique perspective on their most inner and sacred queries, as well as offering possible solutions for many of life's quandaries and hardships. Indeed, when understanding the particulars of each unique problem or condition we face in life, we often need a gentle nudge in the right direction to accomplish our goals. *The Theban Oracle* offers you the unique chance to explore, define, and conquer many of the issues we face daily.

History's most wise and honored within the realms of the collegian, the sage woman, and the magi are exemplified herein in order to pay homage to their noble works and for their contributions, including those more nefarious within the realms of the metaphysical arts and sciences. These luminaries are so honored for the freedom they had to forfeit in order for us to receive such wisdom. Since there are far too many such examples to represent in all, the twenty-four individuals and the one mystery persona I have chosen, the historically elusive "Bethany," have been specifically selected in order to offer a unique and diverse perspective on life and living, including the strengths and weaknesses of these most revered or notorious individuals.

Each luminary represented offers us their individual powers of uniqueness and giving, as well as their earthly mistakes and shortcomings, denoting the human condition that often ruled over them. Each luminary belongs to a specific group of disciplines, wherein each exemplifies the uniqueness of their own knowledge and expertise as presented within their distinctive authority, along with their gifts, strengths, and overall purpose within their particular craft. The adjacent Theban symbol stands for and represents the exemplified persona by action and purpose, encompassing an appropriate angelic caste from the hierarchy of angelic forces, a system that was embraced by Cornelius Agrippa and many other magi and ancient occult philosophers. Consequently, this process and its defined understanding should express to us that even with failure and hardship, there may blossom from within each of us, success and blessings, and a chance to work out our issues in the way of the ancients.

For each luminary exemplified, I relate their historical roles in magick and history, as well as his or her contribution to ancient wisdom. Although the Theban script and its original usage is still a curious subject at best, having no clear or definite history, its powerful reality for many modern practitioners remains a source of inspiration nonetheless. As with other oracles, such as the Norse and Germanic runes, the Celtic Ogham, the Tarot, and other similar implements, this oraclelike gaming system will offer a unique chance to discover personal yet astute answers to everyday issues, as well as serving as a divination process for those so inclined to employ a higher source of wisdom.

Chapter Three

OUTLINE AND GENERAL RULES FOR DRAWING THE THEBAN STONES

Because the keepers of both light and darkness are so important to every form of magick, it is so vital to include the enlightenments of the esoteric within all such works of metaphysics, like that of divination, and like wisdom seeking; therefore, searching for illumination therein . . . I can see such a benefit [magick] with such an endeavor.

REV. DR. SEDGWICK GRANGE, D.SC., CARDIFF UNIVERSITY, WALES, 1914

As with other tools of divination, the rules here are essentially simple. First, it is important to be of stable mind, meaning the feelings one holds within herself will directly convey to the stones, in effect extending to the matrix of the stone itself. If your mind and feelings are that of anger, the response will be one of anger to you. If they are of sadness, the response will in turn be of sadness, so we must remember to use the Theban stones with emotional care, understanding that our own psychic vibrations will naturally fall to the diminutive aspects of the physical medium you will be holding in your hands. As we, like the stones themselves, are all of one body, of one entity we call Mother Earth, it's only natural that one will interact with the other. Spiritually speaking, this is surely the truth.

Second, the stones must remain in a bag or box when not in use. When playing, be sure to take your time, not rushing to pull a stone from the bag. Your hand should be placed within slowly, your fingers gently caressing the stones, in a deliberate manner. Doing so will allow you to feel the right stone for you. Because the ancients believed that all things contain and offer natural energies, essentially there being life within all things, be it the trees, the water, the air, or the earth, the Theban stones are made of such things, therefore they too must have energy, which will both attract and repel equally.

Because the honor roll of history's famous leaders of magick and of the old religions is so extensive, making it literally impossible to credit every such person respectfully, I have listed twenty-four of the most recognized authorities in ancient metaphysics and magick. For example, the great alchemist Paracelsus will represent his most powerful qualities. For instance, "a sacrifice" is the divinatory message for this noted alchemist and physician. As he had made many personal and professional sacrifices during his life, his is the best example to represent zeal, passion, and similar qualities of the human spirit.

Although the oldest and most influential texts on Medieval magick and metaphysics, as well as the many scholars who lay claim to the source of the Theban alphabet and other celestial writings, are in truth unable to pinpoint historical facts, this absorbing mystery of centuries ago is finally put to a decisive and exact position. For the sake of divination and insight, it is applied in the purest form herein. Although it would go beyond the scope of this work as a simple game or divination system to include every detail of such in-depth research, I include various terminologies that will aid in the comprehension of such wisdom for individual insight and future reference.

From King Solomon and Zoroaster, and from Lao Tzu and Joan of Arc, and even the modern practitioners of mundane, low, and high magick, the major elements of understanding the magickal arts— whether it be of the alchemical sciences, spirit conjuring, and divination or the herbalist arts—all have revolved around the heavenly realms and the aid of either angelic or daemonic assistance. Indeed, as the heavens have always played a key role in the science and methodology of all true magick, a simple format is included in this book, in order to give a comprehensive foundation to the overall practice and reality for your spiritual process. And, though the reality of angels and the harbingers of good is seen in practically every culture, the truth of such reality is so vast that it would constitute a scholarly book in itself in order to faithfully represent its proper significance. For the purposes of *The Theban Oracle*, I offer a relatively minor example for the sole purpose of recognition and enticement.

The Process

The process is simple: The player will draw one or more stones from the bag, any of which are suitable for any question asked. When drawing the stones in play, such as the simple one-stone draw, this may signify a challenge for the day or a word of advice. This draw is designed for a single yet meaningful answer for the random thought or query, which lies in one's subliminal mind. The three-stone draw signifies the player's present situation, a challenge or issue to be resolved, and the best process to over-come that situation for a positive resolution. In addition, there are several other stone-drawing options, which will enlighten the spirit and enhance the mystical aspects of the psyche, all designed to further one's spiritual intellect and soulful resolve. It is, how-ever, important for the player to remember above all that she is the true source of this art of divination of what the person is feeling; indeed, their innermost vibrations will manifest in the stones they elect. As many ancient magi and sage women would have known, there are no coincidences in anything we experience or do, so the player should consider the vast uniqueness of the stones they draw.

When you're ready to draw the stones, you will see that this process falls within the *One, Three, Six,* and *Nine* categories, as well as a *Tree of Life* and the ancient *Hand Cast* method. Each will represent a particular answer or aspect of an answer for any specific question you ask. Questions in the form of: "Your present situation and what that situation means in the greater scheme of things . . . " generally show the player what he is experiencing at that present time. Although the answer may indeed offer the player a somewhat cryptic view of their situation, the stone is nonetheless designed to let the player formulate specific answers, themselves finding meaning to each response. If for instance the player draws the *Nostradamus Theban Stone*—which indicates and represents *endurance and steadfastness,* calls for the player to "stay on course," and not to give up no matter how bad the situation currently is—such a response may hold a rather deep and meaningful indication to the person drawing that stone, so be sure to take your time and think about the response presented.

If such a stone is pulled for the "challenge at hand" aspect to the question, it may reflect to the player that he should not change what is currently taking place, no matter how mundane or insignificant the situation may appear. As the possibilities are literally beyond number, such a stone draw will inspire many directions for the player to consider. The following examples represent the means and modality of drawing the Theban stones. You may wish to investigate the following patterns to answer many of life's issues.

THE DAILY DRAW OF ONE

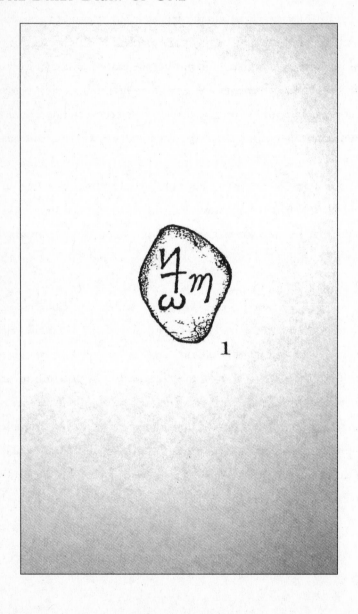

The single stone draw is the most simplistic of all and is meant primarily to be done in the morning, or at the start of your day. However, you may find this form of divination useful for any time or occasion; it is designed to uncover the most meaning in its randomness. Here, the player will have all possibilities, as that particular stone will hold a message that only the person drawing it will understand. Because each stone has a deeply profound meaning and representation, it is important to remember that the significance depends largely on what is already taking place in your life.

If, for example, you were to pick the *Joan of Arc Theban Stone,* which indicates "change," or "a time of journey," then this may tell the person drawing that stone that there is indeed a journey ahead, or that a change in something significant is about to take place. Perhaps there will be a different line of work offered, or you will be taking a figurative journey, perhaps learning something new that will assist you in the future. The prospects are many, but when the player remembers to be aware of his questions, the answers will appear in a significant and personal manner.

THE THEBAN THREE-STONE FORMATION

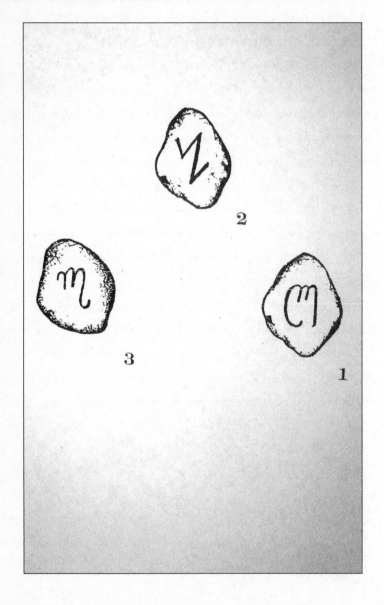

Probably the most universal format used in any divination method, the three-stone draw allows the player to ask a three-part question. Like any good story, there's a beginning, a middle, and an end, and this format is rendered in much the same manner. Like each and every draw, the player must take her time during the process. Unlike the one-stone draw, it is vital that the player not rush for an answer; instead taking time to feel the stones, while at the same time actively, sincerely, and quietly asking a heartfelt question.

Before we begin with the draw, it would be wise to understand the significance of a "triad formation" in relation to the oracle process and certain forms of divinatory magick. Within the realms of ancient magick and within sacred geometry, the triad formation is seen as a fusion of its parts. Beginning with a *monad*, meaning the one, the *dyad*, meaning the second, and the perfect magickal third, the *triad*, this draw rounds out a special formation that represents and creates a sacred position within the universe. Each has been represented with great honor throughout the ages, such as seen within the Christian ideal: the *Father, Son,* and *Holy Spirit.* Because the number three contains such mystical and powerful elements in the occult arts, it is significant in the context of the Theban Oracle.

The ancient Greek scholar, mathematician, and magus Pythagoras believed that the number three was a powerful number, which stood for all working things in the universe, and being of a sacred order. Therefore, the three-stone draw will be in the shape of a triad, always with the point facing upward. Once done, the player will pull out each stone respectfully, and then place a stone beginning from lower right, center high, and then the lower left in the form of a pyramid or an arrowhead. This *triad* signifies *your place at the present time, the personal challenge you are facing,* and *the possible outcome* that will occur as a result of your intervention. If the Theban stone is "faced away" from your view, then it must be read as a *stone in reverse.* A reversal, much like a stone that's face forward, has an equal and quite opposite meaning, yet will apply equally to your query and situation.

The stones you will pull for the Theban Three-Stone Formation should be arranged in the following manner:

1. Your place at the present time

2. The personal challenge you are facing

3. The possible outcome

Here's one example of a three-stone draw: Let's say I'm having difficulty with someone at work, whom I just cannot get along with no matter what. I go to my Theban stones and place my hand around them, gently shifting the stones between my fingers to pick up the energies, and thinking on my dilemma and how best to address it. I'll do this until I find just the right stones. I lay them before me, which read: the *Bethany Theban Stone,* representing the present situation; the *Dr. John Dee Theban Stone,* representing the challenge ahead; and finally the *Johannes Trithemius Theban Stone,* which represents the best foreseen outcome at hand. Understanding the meaning of each stone drawn, the answers might be seen in the following manner: The *Bethany Theban Stone* signifies the unknown. It is a mystery stone, representing, but not limited to the most innate and secret of happenings within our lives. If, for instance, my question is essentially "why" am I having problems with this certain person at work, or "what" can I do about it, I may find that this stone refers to the mystery, that which is so multifaceted in origin, that this problem may have far too many answers to be specific. This may mean that the problem has not yet been played out or that I will need to finish reading all the stones in order to get any assembly for a possible answer.

The second stone, which indicates the challenge at hand, such as an issue you will need to overcome, is the *Dr. John Dee Theban Stone.* This stone signifies concentration and thought, and may simply be telling the person drawing this stone to be still for a moment and think about his situation. Is the situation a true problem at all, or should there be any concern at this point? Again, the answer one might formulate may have vast differentials to an answer you might discover, which simply indicates that each problem will be seen differently from one player to the other. Because Dr. John Dee would have told you to sit a moment and look at your problem, the advice is certainly one of a wise sage: a man who would look at his present situation with great mindfulness and zeal. Certainly, he would not jump to any one conclusion, nor would he make a rash judgment. He would instead actually sit and contemplate his problem and work it out.

As Dr. John Dee was a man having the ear and confidence of England's most celebrated and cherished ruler, Queen Elizabeth I, being fully aware of her temperament and habits, he still managed to speak with quality about her most inner secrets and aspirations, a privilege that very few men had in her presence. Therefore, in relative essence, this stone may be telling you to wait a moment, and not jump the gun. So, you're having a problem with someone from work. Should you get angry with this person and add to the already festering conflict, or should you instead try to work with this person and offer the banner of peace, thus de-escalating the conflict in its entirety? The answer may vary from situation to situation of course, but the general response should seem clear regardless, even if there is more to the situation than meets the eye.

The final stone in the triad formation is the *Johannes Trithemius Theban Stone*, which represents *discipline and self-order*. Johannes Trithemius was the abbot of Sponheim who authored many works on alchemy and high magick. Friend and mentor to Cornelius Agrippa, Johannes Trithemius represents the ancient icon for self-discipline and for having a scholarly sense of order in all that he did. Indeed, he had contributed much to the advances of the metaphysical arts and sciences, yet was challenged with the great egos of his contemporaries, which led many of his humanitarian ideals to go unobserved and unappreciated in his day. In short, the *Johannes Trithemius Theban Stone* may be telling you that similar obstacles and challenges may need to be properly dealt with. Though you understand that there is a conflict, how will you go about it? What can this stone possibly represent for you? Again, because there will always be several ways in which to interpret each stone, you must consider the timeless edict to be still and reflect, to warn of jumping too soon into any situation or conflict.

So, what does it all mean? With these aforementioned stones, I have found and interpreted my own set of answers. *The Bethany Theban Stone*, the unknowing or "mystery," tells me that although there is indeed a struggle taking place, there may be no rhyme or reason to it. This person you're having problems with at work may have issues with no bearing at all on you, meaning that there should be little reason to take offense or be anxious in this conflict or situation. Instead, simply ignore the often annoying shortcomings of others, and look beyond such unfortunate behaviors. Of course, understanding that not all problems will mirror mine or yours exactly, it is important to remember that not all issues are the same in all categories, so interpretations will always vary.

The second stone, the *Dr. John Dee Theban Stone*, represents a challenge that refers to thought and concentration in the context of the Theban Oracle. This stone advises the person drawing it to be mindful of his situation and surroundings, and that this person may need to apply this wisdom before you go any further. Taking these steps may silence one's problems altogether, offering good sense and reflection in the process.

The third stone, representing a possible outcome to the situation, is the *Johannes Trithemius Theban Stone*, which advises one to manifest self-discipline and order within the context of the situation at hand. Doing this will offer the chance to literally sit back and reflect on the situation, and to continue regardless of the hurdles one must first jump in order to make progress. In the end, when following the counsel of this divination process, the person drawing these stones may find that there is indeed good advice in the outcome. This process gently advises to put the affairs at hand in the right order, having the self-discipline to move beyond the little things, and get on with what needs to be accomplished in order to proceed. Naturally, the way we will interpret the answers will vary from issue to issue, but you'll find a unique wisdom in how you decipher the Theban Oracle, and how you will deal with your situations as a result of this process. In short, with just the right amount of thought and soulful reflection on the answers you receive, you're sure to discover the best answers to your queries.

THE THEBAN SIX

Now that you have a general understanding of the stone-drawing process, it's time to ascend to the six-stone draw. Here, much like the aforementioned processes, you will draw in the same manner, but the time for contemplation will require greater tenacity. Basically, as the need for contemplation grows in relation to your question or situation, the necessity for an in-depth manner of questioning is also needed. Here, the *triad formation* will be more akin to the time-honored traditions used by alchemists and sacred geometrical magicians, where the basic elements of the three-stone draw will be divided equally to form a diamond shape. These "triads" will represent part of a mixture, which is designed to accompany another mixture. In this case, the *Upper Triad* represents the most important aspect of the overall question. Here, we see the first three aspects of this draw: *your place at the present time, the personal challenge you are facing,* and *the secondary aspect of that challenge.* The first draw, "your place at the present time," represents where you are spiritually and emotionally. Within the context of the Theban oracle, this stands for where you are as far as your question or situation is concerned.

"The personal challenge you are facing" represents the meat of your situation. Here, the stone you draw will offer a possible rationale for the problem that is challenging you at the time. Remember that such a draw does not represent a definite answer to your situation; it may, however, offer you clues about your situation that may

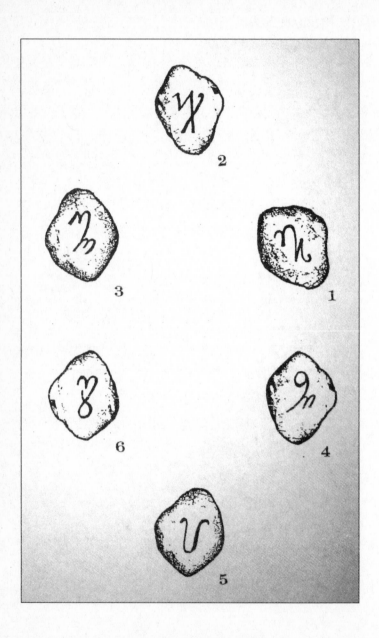

assist you in finding a solution to it. The primary reasoning with this stone, just as with the one-stone draw, is to give you a chance to reflect on and contemplate that stone's meaning. Likewise, the next stone drawn, "the secondary aspect of that challenge," is meant to further the investigation of your situation or problem. This stone will act either as a backup to the previous stone and its meaning or as a second opinion, thus offering you another possible way to look at your situation.

Once the *Upper Triad* is complete, you will move on to the second half of this mixture, which is equally as important, but able to be varied in degrees. The *Lower Triad* represents the next steps you may need to choose to rectify a situation. When this formula is associated within the context of the Theban oracle, the *Lower Triad* regards a series of choices you may need to take as part of your overall divination process. This is called *The Pivotal Option,* and it offers ideas you may wish to consider in order to make changes in your problem or situation. These three Theban stones will represent the crucial aspects of your question. What it reveals in the divinatory reading will offer you diverse advice about your particular question. The next part of the *Lower Triad* is known as *The Bearing,* which represents the current course of your situation and where it may continue to go. In a similar fashion, famed physicist Albert Einstein formulated several notions about the concepts of time travel and the space-time-continuum theory that may exemplify an equivalent here. Einstein's notions about cosmic movement

---

were symbolized by two pieces of driftwood being thrown in a circular-shaped river at the same time. Each piece of wood would always end up at a different location even though they should have arrived together. Equally, in relation to the Theban oracle, the stone that represents *bearing* is much like the driftwood, which may change drastically along the course of the journey. Like the driftwood, which may have been affected by a wave or a gust of wind, your spiritual journey may also be affected by some natural or unnatural event, thus slowing or advancing your journey.

The final aspect of the *Lower Triad* represents *The Best Likely Outcome*. Here, this Theban stone is meant to cast light on the future of your situation. Remember that, much like the piece of driftwood in the river, which will never land on the same shore twice, so true is your own destiny. This Theban stone will offer you insight on where you're heading, what is most likely to take place, and even how you will go about doing it. The answer you may receive the following day, however, may be vastly different because we are all like the driftwood in a continuously moving river of life, within a vast and ever-evolving universe. Though this aspect of the stone-drawing process may at first seem intense, try to remember that the only thing asked of the Theban Six draw is patience, sincerity, and deep contemplation.

The stones you will pull for the Theban Six should be arranged in the following manner:

Upper Triad

1. Your place at the present time

2. The personal challenge you are facing

3. The secondary aspect of that challenge

Lower Triad

4. The Pivotal Option

5. The Bearing

6. The Best Likely Outcome, and Possible Resolution

Each stone will follow in the above example, and will exemplify a deeper understanding of your situation; the gravity of that situation, the unique challenge you will face, and the most likely outcome that you will experience as a result. Understand that how you feel and how you envision yourself and your circumstances, whatever they might be, will surely affect the manner of your draw. Remember, asking meaningful and sincere questions when drawing the stones will offer the most meaningful responses for you.

THE THEBAN NINE

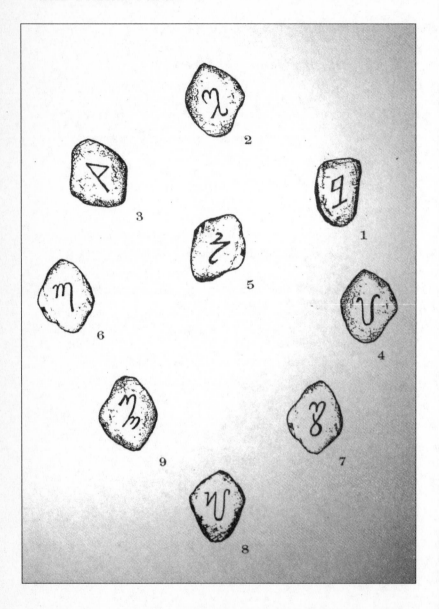

For a further, more meaningful inquiry into your questions, you may deepen the nature of your divination process with this stone draw. The Theban Nine is devised to be set within a "three-tier" format of the triad system—the *Upper Triad*, the *Median Triad*, and the *Lower Triad*. As with the Theban Six stone draw, the nine-stone draw will ask similar questions, such as: *your place at the present time, the main aspects of your personal challenge*, and *a secondary challenge*, though these inquires will be placed within the *Median Triad* section. This is done in order to expand the divination process. The *Upper Triad* begins to look at *Your Past Outlook*, which represents any issue or issues that may be directly affecting your situation or questions. It may also reflect an event that is still playing out in the subconscious, which may be causing a hindrance in your progression.

The *Foundation of the Self* aspect refers to the core foundation of your psyche. Whoever draws this stone will be shown at least an inkling of a possible issue that may be holding a problem in place. This "foundation" may represent an outdated idea or philosophy that has over the years formed into a solid foundation within the psyche, and eventually keeps that persona from progressing in life in a healthy manner.

The last aspect of this *Upper Triad* is the *Ouroboros*, which artistically translates to "the serpent that eats its own tail." Much like what this image implies, the *Ouroboros* stands for the problem that is continuously occurring, never finding full cessation or resolution. If for instance someone is affected by an addiction such as by drugs or alcohol, this person's problem will continue to worsen until he ceases the patterns of that addiction. Like this problem, the *Ouroboros* represents a deep-seated issue that is continuing in cyclic fashion. This stone may represent such an issue and offer a possible idea to change such problematic issues, thus moving forward.

In the case of this Theban stone draw, it is directly related to the *Foundation of the Self* aspect of this triad and shows a possible link between the two, where in essence a psychological and spiritual marriage occurs. When we look at our problems and the innermost secrets that we might be suppressing, and when such issues are deeply buried in the foundations of our subconscious, the need for complete recognition, comprehension, and cessation of such issues becomes clear.

Once you have completed the *Upper Triad,* having made your choices, it is time to draw the *Median Triad.* Like the Theban Six stone draw, there is: *your place at the present time, the main aspect of the personal challenge you are facing,* and *the secondary aspect of that challenge.* Following this, you will complete the process with the *Lower Triad,* which consists of *The Pivotal Option, The Bearing* and *The Best Likely Outcome.* Following the same guidelines as the Theban Six stone draw, you will be afforded a much deeper view of your situation before bringing a close to your divination process.

The stones you will pull for the Theban Nine will be arranged in the following manner:

Upper Triad

1. Your Past Outlook

2. The Foundation of the Self

3. The Ouroboros

Median Triad

4. Your place at the present time

5. The main aspect of the personal challenge you are facing

6. The secondary aspect of that challenge

Lower Triad

7. The Pivotal Option

8. The Bearing

9. The Best Likely Outcome, Possible Resolution

THE HAND CAST

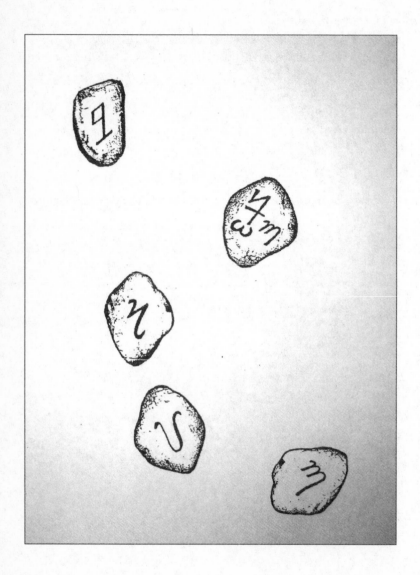

The hand-cast method of divination is likely to be the most traditional in human history. From the ancient soothsayers to the most advanced wizard, one of the more simplistic methods of consulting an oracle has been the hand-casting technique. As simple as can be imagined, the village sage or cunning woman may simply reach into his or her pouch and pull out several stones, shards of wood, or bones, usually with a mystic inscription carved upon them, such as the *runic, cuneiform,* or *Ogham* symbols, and toss them freely to the ground. The extracting of these items from the bag would be done with a swift, deliberate, yet gentle demeanor, usually with that sage chanting softly to encourage the gods for a favorable outcome. In either case, the one drawing the stones in this fashion is doing so to hear what the universe will tell them, whether to proceed or to retreat; the answer would always be taken seriously.

To use the hand-cast method, it is important to remember that there is no "taught" or "designated" method for doing so. Sometimes, the one drawing these stones may pull out three, or four, sometimes even ten or more at one time. There is no line or setup in which to place the stones, nor is there any one way to interpret them. The purpose of the hand cast is to look upon them as a quick response to the chaotic realms of the universe. The often messy arrangements the stones may appear as may suggest many individual and quite personal things. Indeed, some wise men and women who draw in this manner may simply refer to the end product as "in the stars." Basically, the concept of a mass field of stars often relates the appearance of a hand-cast spread, and you may find that the answers you receive in this manner are not only strangely psychic of your question or situation, but also revealing in the answer.

Once you have become acquainted with the Theban alphabet and its meanings and representations, and with added practice, you will no doubt find a clearer, uninhibited picture of the ancient ways of magick. Although immediately suitable for some, this divination process may at first prove a little elusive. Nevertheless, press on with the knowledge that the answer, no matter how hard you try to evade or change it, will always be spiritually motivated for you. You only have to relax and trust in the process. Do this, and a meaningful and enlightened answer will find you.

For this method of Theban divination, you must remember the following rules: First and foremost, you must never throw the Theban stones too hard on any surface, remembering to gently cast the stones, very much like a farmer would sow seeds in a field. A simple toss from right to left or left to right is all that is needed. Second, it would be prudent to cast your stones on a relatively soft surface, such as on carpeted floor or on the face of Mother Earth herself. As with any other drawing method herein, if the stone is symbol side up, simply read it for what that stone is interpreted as. If the Theban letter is facing away from you, showing a blank stone, then it must be read as a *stone in reverse*. If for instance you pull only three or four, or ten or more stones, read them one at a time in any sequence that first comes to mind. Remember, even if there seems to be no rhyme or reason, there is always a purpose for what stones you drew. There are no coincidences in the cosmic scheme of things.

Above all, as with all the stone-drawing methods—minus that of the one stone draw, which is meant to offer a universal morsel of advice for the day—you must always think upon your question with great mental and soulful tenacity. There is no rush to this divination process. Understanding with belief and sincerity that your spiritual vibrations and very essence are being transferred to the mineral stones you are now holding will add to the overall oracle process and create a sense of magickal wonderment that will last for years to come. Because we are made up of the same natural elements that the earth is composed of, it is vital to comprehend that we are connected to the earth, like any other elemental object.

When preparing to use the hand-cast method, you may wish to take your time holding the stones while still in their bag. Wait until the stones are warm in your hands, actively feeling for that psychic bond between you and the stone. Indeed, you will begin to feel a life to the stones as never before, actually being able to pick the right ones specifically for you. Moreover, it is important not to try and feel out the inscriptions on the stones. Instead, let the stones touch the palm of your hand and fingertips, holding and caressing them as if they were tiny, delicate life forms, and then proceed. The result, much like the vast universe, will be mysterious and strangely accurate for you and you alone.

THE TREE OF LIFE

As the Middle Ages brought about the resurgence of many ancient magickal practices, it is paramount to include such aspects of those teachings here. Cornelius Agrippa and his contemporaries explored the many realms of God, the angelic orders, and various mystical traditions throughout their magick-seeking tenures. Of these traditions, the mysteries of the Kabbalah were explored, transferred, and designated to many purposes and stations for the Medieval scholars and magi. Having been created for adjoining many aspects of magick to everyday life, by the 15th century, the meanings of the Kabbalah and its divine properties took on a more consequential state of affairs. Indeed, as Agrippa and others had concentrated on many ancient works of the Kabbalah and similar philosophies, it became necessary to have a basic understanding of ancient Jewish mysticism.

The Kabbalah, literally meaning "receiving," is a lengthy collection of written works and symbolism from the first five books of the Torah. It holds within it the very foundations of all things, of life in the corporeal world and the elemental forces that intertwine and bind all things created by the Almighty, to the most simplistic meanings of our waking state. Indeed, the creator had passed the wisdom of the ages down the course of mankind, beginning with the angels and then unto man, specifically the luminaries of biblical lore. Indeed, King Solomon the wise ruler of the Holy Land is believed to have mastered the Kabbalah in full, thus infusing many of its secrets into

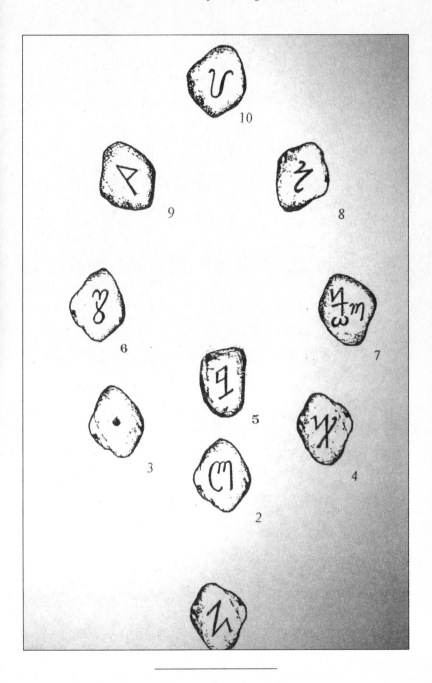

his later literary works: the *Key of Solomon* and the *Lesser Key of Solomon.* And, as such inspired works continue to enthrall modern-day magi, as they teach a steady and meaningful divinity to those who seek their wisdom, the most profound aspect of the Kabbalah is applied in the context of the Theban Oracle: the *Tree of Life.*

The *Tree of Life* represents the very foundation of the continuously working universe and its sacred structure. Beginning from the bottom or "trunk" of this tree, which stands for the base line of all things, it also represents man's place on the spiritual consciousness and order of divine placement in all things. Like climbing a tree, we start from the bottom and work our way upward, hoping to reach the top without falling. In the spiritual sense, man must do this as well, but through trial and error; hoping to reach the top, to one day be with the Almighty in a state of perfection and bliss. Furthermore, the *Tree of Life* spans downward from heaven to form the ethereal emanations known as the *Sefirot,* which are connected to twenty-two entwined pathways throughout the Kabbalah's structure. Each of the *Sefirot* contains a separate significance, with several finite implications within them. With a plethora of both enlightening and cryptic meanings, the *Tree of Life* is an enigmatic yet wonderful creation that has served all forms of magick and elemental wisdom throughout the ages.

Over the centuries, many rabbis and scholars alike have investigated the intrinsic meanings of the symbols used to represent each of the ten icons within the *Sefirot,* as each symbol has a diverse and fundamental meaning; standing for the life-persuading aspects of our growth, and for our desire to be one with the Almighty. Therefore, this exquisite and most revered process is duplicated here, though applied directly in the context of the Theban Oracle.

To begin with, it is important to understand that the format of the *Tree of Life* and its relationship to divination are similar in that each question falls upon one of the ten individual iconic meanings. In so doing, I have placed the individual connotations from bottom to top, all aligned with the divine attributes of the Kabbalah. In applying the Theban stones, each will be read as listed below. For instance, if drawing a stone for the tenth *Sefirot* on the *Tree of Life*, such as the Hebrew representation for *Keter*, which represents the "crown" of the tree, and stands for "happiness," then your answer will reflect how that subject, "happiness," applies to you as you are at the time of drawing the stone.

The use of the *triad* system is still in effect here, with the addition of one "level," which represents the middle level of the *Tree of Life* called the *Median Triad*. It also represents the beginning of your spiritual foundation and what lies beneath, which is not commonly seen by others. Remember that each *Sefirot* will represent an answer for what is occurring in your life at the time of drawing that stone. If your outlook has been soured by sadness or anger, then your outlook is apt to represent such feelings in the stones that you choose.

The stones you will now pull will be arranged in the following manner:

Upper Triad

    10. Happiness (Keter)

    9. Wisdom (Chokmah)

    8. Understanding (Binah)

Median Triad

    7. Love, Compassion (Chesed)

    6. Power, Strength (Gevurah)

    5. Beauty, Harmony, Inner Peace (Tiferet)

Lower Triad

    4. Victory, Endurance (Netzach)

    3. Intellect, Reason (Hod)

    2. The Foundation, Sexuality (Yesod)

    1. The Kingdom, What Lies Beneath (Malkuth)

As you work your way through the *Tree of Life* system, when you're holding the Theban stones in the palm of your hand, envision each topic with as much personal sentiment as you can, knowing that the stones you pick will simply express what your spirit is resonating at that time, in fact, mirroring the way you feel about that question from the innermost aspects of your spiritual manna.

As this is the most advanced system of divination in the context of the Theban Oracle, you may wish to do this stone drawing in private, exploring your question and your personal issues in isolation from others. Because these topics and issues are openly listed in this book, you may not be able to keep your personal answers from others. In addition to privacy, you may find that when this divinatory ritual is performed with the lights low, with a few candles lit, perhaps with incense burning, the atmosphere will elevate the mood to that of a sacred status and offer you a more profound reading.

Chapter Four

CLARIFICATION AND METHODOLOGY OF THE THEBAN ORACLE

N ow we begin with the meanings and clarification of the various Theban stone draws. As there are a series of individual meanings in the context of the Theban Oracle, you should familiarize yourself with each of the Theban symbols before you get started. Moreover, when reading about the stone that you have just drawn, it would be prudent to begin by reading the entire passage listed for each definition, as each will have a unique tie-in with the other stones pulled. After a while, you'll begin to memorize the passage's meanings as a whole, simply referring to the abridged subtitle, its significance, and the annotated divinatory meaning that lies just below it.

Reading each Theban stone's passage is relatively simple. For instance, if you draw the *Joan of Arc Theban Stone,* you will see the subtitle: *The Journey Ahead, Change* and *a New Development.* These abbreviated meanings will offer you a simple answer once you have become completely aware of the entire divinatory passage and its meaning, which will become clearer the more you play. When drawing the Theban stones for others, you may wish to read the divinatory meaning in full, so as to explain their situation as only they will understand it. Also, because each and every question is of a personal nature, it may be best to allow that person the anonymity in their queries, letting them keep their questions private. When doing so, the person drawing the stones will find a unique comfort level that will only add to the overall divinatory process.

Once again, as with any tool of divination, it is important to remember that the one asking the questions must ask from her or his heart, always to identify the most sincere of questions. Because the answers to these divinatory meanings are designed to offer a deep reflection of your innermost queries, honesty is always the principal ingredient. Moreover, it is important not to force the one drawing the stones to hurry, nor to help answer for them. Because each of these stones has a deeply personal representation and meaning, we must respect and appreciate each individual's choice of when and how to interpret the stones.

When you are ready to begin the divination process, whether for yourself or for a group of friends, remember that the space you will be doing this in must be a quiet, tranquil place, a sacred space. Although we may not always have this option, we may at least "ground" the area and the people involved, giving them the sense of serenity and protection. To do this for the process of divination or simply to add the cosmic and spiritual energies to all our endeavors, I use the "White Light of Protection" method. This simple spiritual cleansing process will have the individual form a cup with his hands, then hold the cupped hands over the head of oneself or another with eyes closed, visualizing a whitish-blue glowing energy within the hands. Then, this person will slowly open each of the fingers, draping the body or location in a meaningful and direct fashion, spreading this unseen "magick light of protection" around you and your location.

When performing this task, you might wish to make a verbal decree, such as "May the white light of the heavens protect me and all I do from harm and negativity, with my faith, with my love, my honor, I so decree it, and make it so." This process will secure your belief that the good within the universe will watch over and protect you while performing such a ritual, or even when involved with everyday life. As this invisible energy is literally the very proto-matter of the ethereal realms, its protective barrier over an individual or location will decrease the possibility of negativity, psychic attack, or even psychic vampirism, which is the intentional or unintentional draining of another's energy and positive emotions through psychic means. Though sounding a bit supernatural, it was a well-known concept among the ancients, and continues to be a subject of importance for contemporary magi as well.

The following section characterizes each individual Theban letter, the corresponding luminary, and an individual message with deep meaning. Each is designed to sum up the player's significant purpose in a particular situation, a problem, or a question that will only be understood by the one drawing that lettered stone.

Remember, taking the time to draw each stone, and then contemplating it deeply and soulfully, will always bring about an equally deep answer or set of answers. So, when engaged in your divinatory quest, know that without patience and honesty, your answer will glean the same in return. May the wisdom of the ancients favor you.

𝖞

The Journey Ahead, Change, a New Development

JOAN OF ARC (1412–1431)

This Theban stone is personified by the will and determination of *Joan of Arc,* also known as Jeanne d'Arc, and the Maid of Orléans. This peasant girl, who by the age of seventeen would lead the French military to many victorious campaigns, and would do so at the cost of her life, represents innocence and compassion, as well as the divine tenacity and personal drive that personifies the meaning of this Theban stone. Although Joan of Arc was in truth no practicing witch or dabbler in the dark arts, she is believed to had been psychically in tune with many things of a preternatural nature, as well as having conversed with the Almighty through clairaudient means. She will always be remembered for her willingness to go where none other dared go, and for having true faith in her beliefs, regardless of the consequences from both her enemies and her benefactors.

Known for winning many victorious battles, and for her desire to fight against the injustice of her enemies and the wickedness of her people, she soon became a nuisance to both court and king. She would dare to wear the clothing of men and speak proudly of her devotion to God, but her zeal and candor only culminated in the accusation of witchcraft, believed to have been prompted and advised by daemons and darker influences than that from God. In the end, Joan of Arc would become one of the millions throughout the ages to be taken by the fires of lies, hatred, and ignorance. Like the thousands who would join her, she too had a journey to partake in, a journey that will be represented as a sacred path of new choices and beginnings.

DIVINATORY MEANINGS

Like the fledgling passage this enchanted child undertook, this stone represents the beginning of a new journey and a new path, which is the very essence of moving from the old to the new. Think of its meaning as the driftwood that travels in a stream: though its destination that cannot be determined with perfect accuracy, it still has a purpose. Such a destination may give credence to where you may end up in the cosmic setting, but trust and patience is in order here. Indeed, the wisest of men and women may not fully know their destination, merely the path they might take. This stone tells that a journey lies ahead, that one must begin from the beginning, and that all things begin anew.

Much like the thoughts, the dreams, and the aspirations we all have in our lives, this stone signifies that there is not only a need for constant movement, but also a need for constant change. When this stone is drawn, it may signify that you too must submit to the natural pull of what is taking place in your life. Remember, young Joan went from peasant girl to a general and religious icon, to a heretic and witch all within the space of a few short years. It was during this ever-changing growth that she would sadly witness the lack of true feelings and honesty from her leaders, and even her king, once her benefactor and confidant. In the end, Joan's life would be forfeited, dying at the hands of her enemies as a result of man's greed and treachery.

Although this stone does not necessarily mean that you will end like the heroic Joan of Arc, it does, however, signify that personal change is close at hand. There may be an ending to a relationship or personal situation. While in such moving transitions, remember to remain ever vigilant of modesty and boldness. Much like the mortal personification of this Theban symbol, Joan of Arc, with all her wisdom and compassion for the freedom of her people, and her love for her God, would eventually concede to her passions, and ultimately to the impious ignorance of her enemies. Like this brave soul, you too may become the victim of an untamed passion while on your journey. Like the tide or undercurrent of the great oceans, you too must learn to ebb and flow; follow the natural pulling and pushing, and let that which must be, simply be. Therefore, like the aforementioned driftwood, go where your natural instinct is guiding you, and arrive where the cosmic waters take you. Within this journey, a lesson awaits.

A Stone Faced in Reverse

If you should find this stone turned away from you, it may signify a hindering in the right choices you should be making. Simply put, you will need to pull back the blockages that may stand before you, most likely created over the many years, being placed there as a protective barrier against immaturity or doubtful behaviors. Now is the time to find a new path and let go of such childish fears and shortcomings, by opening the self to the new experience. Therefore, it will be important to "let go and let be," as this is the only path to freedom and understanding.

This Theban stone in reverse suggests that you look deeply within the old pathways most familiar to you. Try to recognize the many obstacles and holes that have always been there. Try to move those obstacles and fill the holes before you proceed any further. Doing so will ensure a safe passage should you choose to remain on that path. Not taking care of such obstacles and holes will only warrant a continuing pattern of failure and stagnation, so be mindful of this journey. Remember what it shows you.

ꝗ

Intellect, Pride, Divine Wisdom, Abundance

KING SOLOMON (970—926 BC)

The son of King David, the great leader of ancient Israel, *King Solomon* was known for his impeccable wisdom, amazing mystical possessions, extreme might, and keen military knowledge. He was also known for his abundance of pride, and the associated shortcomings that coexist with such attributes. This Theban stone represents the modality of thought and mind, of reason and intellectual strides. This stone tells that a fulfillment of some magnitude is inevitable, that somewhere advancement waits. But know that with such advancements come responsibility and purpose. There are no coincidences or mistakes, as in the cosmic scheme of things, all things happen with reason and purpose. Whether as a gift or earned, all things have a reason for occurring.

King Solomon was indeed a brilliant soul, and is remembered for his great deeds in politics, for being the architect of great temples, and as a master of the Kabbalah. Yet, though he had ruled his land for more than four decades, having been advisor to scholar and peasant alike, he found himself so high and so revered that he did not notice the thin veil that he stood upon. After fostering wisdom from angels and daemons alike through the means of arcane magick and necromancy, the mighty king would fall short in the end, for not even his mighty armies, his ornate temples, nor his masses of gold and riches could redeem his once envied stance.

Though little remains of his once vast empire, his legend lives on. Through the will to fight and survive, his offspring continue to cherish the wisdom and fortitude of this most high king of antiquity. As a leader and icon of the Jewish people, his intellect and mental devices, as well as his general humanity, continue to offer the wise an example to respect and a lesson.

DIVINATORY MEANINGS

The *King Solomon Theban Stone* refers to a gain at hand, that there is a gift heading your way in one form or another, either large or small. However, it warns of the misuse by the one who will profit by such gain. It offers the wisdom to the one who draws this stone to be aware that arrogance and pride can only inspire the weak-minded and frayed soul. Caution is the first and foremost step to take now, no matter what gift or gain finds its way to you.

The advice of this Theban stone simply warns not to lack good judgment. It instructs us to be mindful of our thoughts of self-righteousness and unhealthy self-importance. It reminds us to be ever so conscious of our fortunes and advanced states, and to give of ourselves to those who cannot have what we are so fortunate to possess.

This stone may also indicate our deliberate reluctance to choose wisely our path in life, whether it be toward one of great wealth or wisdom. It tells us not to judge and look down on those who have less, or those in a lesser station within our material world. To this end, refer to the gains and losses of such a mighty king and learn what he had to forfeit in the name of wisdom and avarice. Although King Solomon was highly successful in many aspects of his life, he was nonetheless flawed in others. Because love is a vital foundation of true wisdom, as well as of the human condition as a whole, we can see that the relationship here is also one of divine understanding. When drawing this stone, we must earnestly endeavor not to find ourselves too wise or too eminent.

A Stone Faced in Reverse

If you draw the *King Solomon Theban Stone* faced away from you, it signifies that a present issue you're dealing with may become out of control. The bearer of this stone is one who is searching for some form of gratitude or reward. Be it at the workplace, at school, or within the family circle, there is a deep wanting. This stone may also indicate that you will soon become in touch with the darker aspects of your self-image, your pride, or the way you think others see you. Take heed of this, because if you choose to ignore what is being presented to you, the truth of that situation and the method of dealing with it wisely may become lost.

The advice of this reversed stone explains that intense self-reflection is needed. Be wise in the mannerisms you show to others, be prudent in the words and actions you choose, and above all, look honestly into yourself, as the image you think everyone else holds of you may in fact be vastly different. As a judicious professor once instructed: "It is a wise man [or woman], who remains still and observes, while it is a fool who chatters and condemns others." Although this philosophy is indeed prudent for the recent occasion, it certainly stands as sound advice for all regardless.

ᛗ

An Inner Power, Self-Realization, Divine Understanding

ZOROASTER (C. 628–551 BC)

Zoroaster, also known as Zarathustra, was high priest, prophet, religious reformer, and magus in the kingdom of the ancient Perso-Iranian people during the Achaemenidae to the Sassanid periods. Although the exact time and placement of this magus is at best speculative, most scholars believe that he lived around 300 years before the conquest of Alexander the Great. With his mysterious and highly moralistic nature in a time of turbulent ideologies and devastating wars, it is difficult to comprehend the true veracity of such a wise demeanor in an epoch of violence and confusion. Outside of the written documentation that is accepted by most scholars, which tells of a deeply contemplative nature, as well as a wise and gentle approach to living, Zoroaster stood for reason in an age of madness. For this reason alone, the *Zoroaster Theban Stone* represents *an inner power* and *divine understanding* in the context of the Theban Oracle.

Throughout the ages Zoroaster has been thought of as one of the greatest and most mysterious magi to ever have lived. Indeed, it is his mystery that has inspired such philosophers as Kant, Diderot, and Voltaire to write of the power of his legend and philosophical views, and it was this ancient magus who motivated Mozart to immortalize mystical aspects in his opus *The Magic Flute*. By the 18th century, Zoroastrianism saw a grand rebirth in many Western cultures, and the philosophies of Zoroaster continue instructing us to think before we act, and to show compassion even in times of stress and turbulence.

DIVINATORY MEANINGS

The *Zoroaster Theban Stone* represents the embodiment of self-realization and of celestial understanding. It specifies that the path you are presently on must be continued, and that you are becoming a spiritual warrior who must follow where you are being drawn to. There are no mistakes here; simply trust the path that is showing itself to you.

As the great magus Zoroaster fostered the reformation of the soul, and taught that wisdom is best found within, it is this credo that must be pursued now. You are on a divine quest that will offer sweet fruits when first you deeply contemplate and pursue pure mindfulness. If you stay on this spiritual path, you will glean the wisdom of divine understanding. And though there may be a few bumps and bruises along the way, stay on course regardless. In the end, while the rest of the world is losing its cool, you will remain inwardly calm, thus projecting the aura of the wise and content sage.

You are seeking wisdom now, and for a wholeness that has been missing in your life. You're searching for an inner power that will confirm your own acceptance of self-reliance and self-worth, waiting for peace and truth to materialize in the process. Although you already possess these attributes by nature, they may be a little scored and frayed by our turbulent and angry world. And even if you're hiding these innermost insights from yourself and others, you're beginning to know the truth now. It's time to contemplate your issues and situations, and be mindful of the best suited mental aspects for securing and repairing what may be vexing you. Concentrate on the rewards you so richly deserve, and they will appear before you.

This Theban stone offers the counsel of contemplation, for realizing the innermost wisdom that is already within you. For the divine understanding of all things, the simple edict of contemplation must be observed with great vigor and intent. It's time to slow down, sit back, and think. You are on the path of the spiritual warrior.

A STONE FACED IN REVERSE

If you draw the *Zoroaster Theban Stone* faced away from you, it shows that you may be making hasty choices in your actions, or otherwise not paying attention to details in your life. In order for you to defeat the negative aspects of your situation, you must first think about what that situation is through and through, and then make sure you understand what it's all about and if it's even worth your efforts. Because only you know what's going on right now, only you can give power to your choices through sincere contemplation and self-realization.

This reversed stone indicates that there is a roadblock in your life, a roadblock that can be either removed or avoided. Only you know what this means as it pertains to your current issues. Listen for that inner voice that you have been ignoring, and look for that morsel of clarity within the dense forest of confusion that is now surrounding you. Simply contemplate and remember that without deep deliberation in your contemplation, you stand to lose what you have been trying to obtain. Simply said, let the madness and turmoil of everyday life pass you by, restricting aggression and anger, regret and hopelessness, and just relax.

♏

Self-Restraint, Reflection, Flow, Transformation

NOSTRADAMUS (1503–1566)

Nostradamus, also known as Michel de Nostradame, is likely to be history's most famed clairvoyant and prophet. An authority in astrology and astronomy, as well as being a noted physician, Nostradamus was able to use his knowledge of science and arcane understanding of the occult to interpret the visions he received in the privacy of a hidden domicile. Predicting the French Revolution, the tyranny of Adolph Hitler, and the assassination of American President John F. Kennedy, this prophet is viewed as the quintessential icon of foresight and divination. Distinguished through his 942 enigmatic quatrains or "centuries," Nostradamus had forewarned the world of the many future hardships, as well as victories, for centuries to come, enthralling generations of researchers in the process.

During his life, Nostradamus suffered many an adversary from colleague to king, but with his keen sense and understanding of the human condition, he was able to employ a scholarly sense of self-restraint with the wisdom he held, and escaped the many inquisitions that were constantly arising throughout Europe. Through an almost divine understanding of reflection, he was able to know exactly what to do and how best to live his life. Indeed, though Nostradamus was certainly entitled to pride and eminence, he chose to remain still and reflect, placing himself in the annals of noble humility and honor for all times.

DIVINATORY MEANINGS

This Theban stone foretells that there are obscure forces at work now, forces of a creative fluidity, where much like the mighty ocean tides, something within you is surging. Indeed, there is an upwelling taking place now, a surge that either can create a spiritual river that will spread this creative fluid to all aspects of your life, or will eat away at the foundations of old and outdated belief systems. Either way, the force of this inner surge is in motion now.

This stone's attributes regard the emotional states of family, romantic relationships, and future vocations. The *Nostradamus Theban*

Stone tells of a great experience soon to arise in your life. A new love, a career change, an extension to your family, or a graduation from the old to the new: in one way or another, there is a substantial change on the way now. This stone counsels that there is also a need for the satisfaction of your innermost emotions: the secret you. Now is the time for emotional and spiritual transformations. There is a call for inward reflection and self-understanding. These attributes are needed before any gainful outcome can be achieved. Therefore, it is necessary to promote the first quality of this stone's essence, *self-restraint,* before you proceed in any of your issues now. Once done, you will begin to see subtle yet rewarding outcomes to your efforts and sacrifices.

A Stone Faced in Reverse

When the *Nostradamus Theban Stone* is faced away from you, it warns that you are not partaking in honest self-reflection. It may be that you are simply not listening to your inner voice or that you're turning away from the self-image that is seen in the mirror of your mind. Now is the time to get honest with yourself and patiently search for those aspects that are keeping you in place. Because this Theban stone also refers to the fluid movements of all things, it may suggest that you are not letting what is needed to naturally take place. To this end, if you are not reflecting on your life in all its capacity, you may be missing something important. The time is vital to take a hard look at yourself; inwardly, soulfully, and most of all, honestly.

𝔏

Friendship, Distinguished Companionship, Partnership

PETRUS DE ABANO (1250–1366)

Petrus de Abano, also known as Peter of Apponus, was one of Italy's most illustrious historical figures. As a philosopher, astrologer, and physician, he was one of the most venerated scholars of arcane wisdom of his day. Having been a collector of rare works on magick, a contributor and accomplished visionary within the ceremonial arts, as well as a kind benefactor for many learned scholars of his day, Petus de Abano is remembered for his desire to drive away the hateful aspects of the Church through divine wisdom and tolerance. He is considered by most scholars of the magickal arts to have been one of the first visionaries to offer respect and brotherly love in a time of irrational upheaval. For this reason, this patron of the mystical arts falls within the domain of friendship and distinguished companionship in the context of the Theban Oracle.

Petrus de Abano, suspected of daemonic conjuring, was persecuted by the holy inquisition. He was imprisoned—his accusers charging him with being a practitioner of the black arts—and subsequently forced to publicly deny the existence of spirits and angels. Although his true crime was his compassion for others, he was labeled a heretic and an enemy of the Church, and so sentenced to die on the fiery pyres. Before the angry mobs were able to carry out their cruelty, however, the once famed and loved physician and scholar died while incarcerated, thus robbing the wicked of their evil lust for blood.

Even in death Petrus de Abano was pursued by his enemies, who wanted to remove his corpse from sacred grounds only to be burned in the streets as an evil wizard. Thankfully, his kindness and goodly contributions were not forgotten by his friends and students, and though his body was moved time and time again, from tomb to tomb, and from graveyard to secret hiding place, he finally found rest in a nameless burial place on the grounds of the ancient St. Augustin's Church in Rome, Italy. Though there is no epitaph or mark of honor for his mortal remains, his name and place in the chronicle of the wise is secured nonetheless.

DIVINATORY MEANINGS

The *Petrus de Abano Theban Stone* indicates that a divine union is close at hand. An addendum to this divine union or partnership, whether it be romantic, platonic, or professional, is that you will not allow yourself to become an underling in that union. Simply said, for this union to work, it is important to remain the individual that you are. Do not assimilate or conform to any person or group of people, as this will take away or reduce the unique nature that surrounds you, thus diminishing or destroying the good that you might experience. Simply be who you are.

Because this Theban stone expresses and represents the separate and unique aspects of the spiritual individual, it is vital to remember that some element of your being will attract, and be attracted to, another outside or opposite element. Just like ingredients that are used for cooking, it is often the differentials of such ingredients and their measurements that make the finished dish a culinary delight. This oracle counsels that you stay on course, allowing your new experiences to take place and remain steadfast throughout all you see, hear, and feel, regardless of your emotions of elation or joy, or when pursued by adversaries and naysayers. Be open to friendship and love, and embrace divine companionship and partnership with honesty and understanding. Now is the time to trust completely in what will soon arrive.

A STONE FACED IN REVERSE

If you find this stone faced away from you, it relates the possibility of two separate issues. The first issue relates that you may be unaware of this proposed union and inadvertently pass it by. You may have become so accustomed to doing things and living your own way that the gift of union may seem illogical or invisible to you. Spiritually open yourself up and listen with that unseen sense and watch how this miraculous experience virtually unfolds for you. Listen with your psychic ears.

The second issue relates that there may be the possibility that a disruptive "union" is approaching. Like the Yin and the Yang, there is darkness within the light and a light within the darkness; both almost always coexist together. This may refer to a relationship, whether it's romantic, a friendship, or a business opportunity that may prove to be overly taxing for you. Perhaps there's a person or situation, even though seemingly friendly and beneficial, that may nonetheless be draining you of your psychic energies. If left untreated, such a union may eventually affect your entire emotional and physical being.

The reversed stone suggests that look deeply within your present situations, and sample the waters before you continue along this life path. Although this may echo a stern warning, it should be taken as good advice for all upcoming affairs.

A Warning, Fear, Ignorance Self-Loathing

JOHANNES FAUSTUS (C. 1480–1540)

The legendary name *Johannes Faustus* is immortalized by the Elizabethan playwright Christopher Marlowe, who tells of a man who sold his soul to a crafty devil named Mephistopheles. For the gaining of love, earthly powers, and great riches, this ignorant necromancer wagered all that he had in the name of avarice and low self-worth. Although this tale enthralled and mystified the people of England and Europe during the late 16th century, the story does indeed have its origins in fact. What has become deeply rooted in European mythology, the Faustus legend, though dramatically embellished and retold in many traditions, is believed to be centered around a living man, a bookbinder and calendar maker named Dr. Johann Faust who lived in Heidelberg during the early part of the 16th century.

Although detailed facts about this man are not entirely clear, oral tradition tells us that he began to refer to himself as "the prince of necromancers," while others simply considered him to be nothing more than a vagabond rogue and teller of many falsehoods. Yet, necromancer or not, Johann Faust became feared as a magician of the black arts, who made many flagrant attempts to wager his soul for material objects and for the love of young women. Indeed, as making pacts with daemons was common knowledge in the folklore of the day, it may not have been unlikely for this unwise necromancer to have had some understanding of the diabolical arts. With such infamous tomes as *The Grimorium Verum* and the alleged tome of the "black pope," the *Grimoire of Honorius*—both which give detailed instructions for summoning daemons and devils, as well as how to trade one's soul for earthly riches—the mentality and mannerisms of this historically elusive figure become clear.

Johannes Faustus represents the sad and fearful far more than simply evil. Though such a man may have had dealings with the darker aspects of the magickal arts, it is highly unlikely that he made benefited from his actions. Where honesty, hard work, and respect for others have painted the long and tedious trail of men and women's sufferings for their faith, this Theban example represents the unfortunate rationale and the desire to succeed through less than honorable methods. The *Johannes Faustus Theban Stone* represents the embodiment of self-motivated failure, the lack of personal faith, and self-loathing, as well as the unfortunate hold that ignorance and greed has over us all. It stands for fear, which forces us to look for the quick and easy path to fortune and glory, which almost always ends with cataclysmic returns.

DIVINATORY MEANINGS

This Theban stone is concerned with the inner communiqué, which is calling upon you now. It indicates that there is something going on in your life that reflects a duality. Because there appears to be two separate fundamentals occurring within a single circumference of a particular issue, you are advised to look within. Like Faustus, you may be approached by various inner desires that may have you imagining about doing what is normally unthinkable from your philosophical point of view. You must remain steadfast in your convictions now, as making the wrong choice may create dire circumstances for you.

As Faustus represents the embodiment of self-motivated failure, reflecting a lack of personal faith, accompanied by a good dose of self-aversion, it stands to reason that if you let this internal fear control your passions now, you stand to lose all that you have fought for. Avoid the quick and easy path to fortune and fame, as such will only lead to negative consequences.

In a quick overview of this oracle, it may be said that inward renovation is in place here. The quest for such transformations, which may translate to throwing out the bad idea in favor of the good, is in full force. Pertaining to your particular issue or situation, you may wish to think twice about the approaching choices that exist, or will present themselves soon. Knowledge and acceptance of your inner self-worth and value is paramount here. Have faith and love for yourself, as nothing will go favorably for you until you do. Simply trust in your initial instincts and follow your gut feeling. You already know the right choices to make.

A Stone Faced in Reverse

When receiving this Theban stone faced away from you, you are asked to be especially mindful of your personal relationships, whether it be friends, lovers, or business partners; you must apply all your honest efforts now. It appears that fissures are forming in your life now. In order to seal these soulful cracks, you are advised to step back and think this situation through. Understand that great efforts are required in order to repel the negativity that is forming in you now. Even if you feel pressured to do something you truly do not wish to do, take the safer route and avoid that which stands before you. Take your time in giving your answers now, as someone may be taking advantage of you, either knowingly or not.

Now is the time to be cool in your demeanor and outward passions. Make sure you maintain a good sense of humor about the issues presented before you. No matter what, how you make your final choice is really up to you regardless of what the opposition says. Although you may know what is needed now, you may be lulled into suspending your initial intentions. Go with what your good judgment tells you, trust in your heart that the right choice is what the opposition denies, and stand by that choice. In the end, you'll be glad you did.

Though what will appear to be stepping back and stepping down from where you once stood—which may also seem to generate many detours, disorder, and even failure—your steadfastness will in fact create more opportunity and respect for your scruples, and foster a positive atmosphere to your character in the process. Simply said, do not give in to the crafty little Mephistopheles who is showing itself to you now. Whether this devil is a man, a woman or is represented as an issue, situation, or business offer, think twice before committing to what your heart has reservations about. The phrase for you now is "To thyself be true."

ᚢ

*The Sovereign Feminine Spirit, Inward Wisdom,
the Pursuit of Enlightenment*

HYPATIA OF ALEXANDRIA (C. 370–415)

The ancient scholar *Hypatia of Alexandria*, the renowned astronomer, mathematician, and Platonic philosopher, serves as the sovereign feminine spirit in the context of the Theban Oracle. With such an eminence of mind and statehood, as well as for her vast virtues of wisdom, Hypatia exemplifies wisdom and the search for enlightenment. Because she was a woman of authority, as well as a pagan in a time when Christianity was beginning to dominate religion, her legend grew within the space of her own time. Moreover, the fact that her status was one of kindness and wisdom, which was elevated during a time of religious intolerance, it's clear that her noble qualities were great in all arenas of her station.

Author of such works as the *Commentary on the Arithmetica of Diophantus* and *A Commentary on the Conics of Apollonious,* as well as being the chief editor of her father's literary works on the *Almagest of Ptolemy,* her wisdom was well acknowledged throughout the civilized world. As her status as a sage woman grew, so did her reputation for overshadowing her male colleagues. And with this, it was only a matter of time until those jealous of her high state and intelligence would plan against her.

Hypatia of Alexandria stands for the highest in free thinking in the ancient world, and for contemporary women who struggle for freedom and equality. Her pursuits and honest inquiry into the realms of mathematics, the sciences, and philosophy have benefited all of humanity. The simple fact that she was female was the intolerable characteristic, especially for those who would demand a man's world alone. Because of this, her many gifts and contributions would remain invisible in the sight of ignorance, judgment, and hate. In the end, Hypatia was accosted by Christian monks for her sins of heresy and for being in league with things other than that of the Church. She was seized, beaten, and dragged to a holy place, where she was mutilated, her flesh ripped from her, and finally burned on a blazing pyre.

Hypatia's love of knowledge and her pursuit of learning and teaching, along with the desire to worship in a manner she felt best, were her only transgression. Yet her integrity and steadfast demeanor made her a legend, and her presence would elevate her to become a silent martyr for all women who truly search, regardless of the barriers that stand before them. Integrity and tenacity encompass these particular aspects of the female spirit, and so represent the entire whole of the feminine circumference in the context of the Theban Oracle.

DIVINATORY MEANINGS

The *Hypatia Theban Stone* represents the uniquely defined female aspect within all of us who pursues wisdom and enlightenment despite insurmountable odds. It is also the intuitive feature of a woman's spirit, which in ancient times was believed to have been inspired by the moon and all things within nature. This stone stands for the woman as a whole, as well as favorable qualities in all people in one form or another.

Because this Theban stone is associated with good women and men and for instilling courage and righteousness in times of great need, it is a significant element throughout the many individual realms of the human condition, making it powerful in the context of the Theban Oracle. When this stone is drawn, it is likely that there are, or will be issues regarding harmony, or for the harmonizing within a personal relationship. It may also represent the need for adjusting to what is new in the realm of such things. This stone exemplifies the need and desire to give and share, which embraces the motherly aspects of the natural female structure. It also expresses a strong yearning to be needed or desired, whether romantically or within the world family community. You are searching now, wanting to be both full and empty at the same time.

Like the ill-fated Hypatia, you have a desire to offer and to teach, but also to take and receive. This is the natural order of things. Sadly, not all are willing to understand or accept such wisdom, and that issue is going to stand in your way now. Be patient, but be firm in what you need to do. Surrender to no one, as the true female spirit is in all of us regardless of gender. Indeed, *Hypatia Theban Stone* is a powerful stone as it denotes a time of liberation, joyfulness, and a distinctive chance to both give and receive. Drawing this stone means that you now have the strength and wisdom to achieve your goals, to complete what needs to be completed, and to find a solution to a problem that stands before you.

A STONE FACED IN REVERSE

If this stone is drawn faced away from you, it signifies an unwillingness to take a particular challenge. There is denial, or perhaps you feel now is not the time to act on something. Perhaps, but unless you clear this blockage, your journey cannot proceed. This reversed stone indicates that you must first relinquish old habits; even if they feel like a safe harbor for you, you must let go. Whether within a romantic or platonic relationship, it's time to look deeply within now. Is it time for a change? In the context here, the oracle advises that the time for emptiness must be accomplished, much like the vessel or crucible must first be emptied before it can be filled again.

Ψ

Concentration, Thought, Wise Decisions

DR. JOHN DEE (1527–1608)

Dr. John Dee, renowned scholar, alchemist, mathematician, astronomer, and astrologer, trained and competent in the Neoplatonic,
Kabbalah, and Hermetic philosophies, and who honorably served
under Queen Elizabeth I, represents concentration, thought, and
wise decisions in the context of the Theban Oracle.

In spite of being a learned man of great magnitude, the wise
doctor was challenged with continuous strife throughout his life.
While prudent in most aspects of deep and studious thought,
he was nonetheless lacking in vital areas of his mundane reality,

such as time, financial, and management issues. Like the preverbal absent-minded professor, he saw to his research and studies of the preternatural and magickal far more favorably than to the more earthly issues of everyday life.

Throughout his professional career Dr. John Dee made his share of bad choices. Though most regarded poor money management and scheduling, he also lacked good social judgment, which sometimes left him looking much less than he truly was. When he met up with Edward Kelly, a bad-tempered Irish charlatan, their union would prove to be both beneficial and dangerous, and always troubled. Indeed, Dee's seemingly unending trust in Kelly's schemes often created more problems than benefits.

During the height of their relationship, Dee and Kelly journeyed across the continent conducting divinatory readings and horoscopes for royal families and nobility. Using Enochian spirit magick and angelic counsel, the two fared well for a time, but would eventually part ways due to debt issues and poor money management. In the end, Dr. John Dee returned to England alone, picking up where he left off, and continued to prosper under Queen Elizabeth I until the end of her reign. He married three times and fathered eight children, served as warden of Christ College in Manchester, and wrote seventy-nine manuscripts on magick and angelic communication. After the death of Queen Elizabeth in 1603, serving a short time under the reign of a new king, Dee fell out of favor with the modern court and was forced to retire penniless and spiritually broken. Like many visionaries before him, he left a wide body of wisdom for the ages, which continues to inspire and enthrall. And, though naïve in some areas of his life, which ended in solitude and poverty, his reputation for being an astute and able man lingers on, continuing to instruct novice and master alike.

DIVINATORY MEANINGS

The *Dr. John Dee Theban Stone* represents the very essence of contemplation, good thought, and wise decision making. Though we may make studious choices in our affairs and be thought of as wise by our contemporaries, we may nonetheless wear the self-made blinders of ignorance that hinder our path in life. While Dr. John Dee was certainly wise and honest in his thinking processes, he lacked two vital elements to his genius: common foresight and mindful consideration.

This Theban stone indicates that there may be mental blocks in your path, those invisible obstacles and potholes that make us stumble and occasionally fall. Yet, with good mental fortitude and proper decision making, you can be victorious in your endeavors. Now is the time for divine patience, as even the most educated and experienced woman or man may occasionally be taken for the fool. Beware the spiritual footing you are treading on. Be always alert for those outside your personal interests and well-being. Instead of becoming too analytical or even paranoid by this assertion however, try sitting back and observe the smallest aspects of those around you. Do you see sincerity or fraudulence?

Although Dr. John Dee was known for his mental magnitude, even he was taken for the proverbial ride by Edward Kelly, the smooth-talking huckster with a few tricks up his sleeve. Make sure when entering any relationship or contract that you take your time in every aspect of its existence. Look it over, and be sure you understand everything about it before you commit. Someone may be watching you now, so stay alert.

This Theban counsel tells you to not be overly enthusiastic in pressing forward too fast or without good judgment. Step back and wait for the signs that will soon appear before you. If this relates to a relationship, either romantic or otherwise, bide your time and be patient, as this act will prove the most prudent for you now, and may indeed flush out the impatient scoundrel that lurks at your door.

A Stone Faced in Reverse

When this stone is drawn faced away, it warns that there is a presence outside the protective barrier that binds your natural persona. Here, you must act rationally and not emotionally. This stone, when reversed, warns that someone is looking for an opening, or that there's a fracture in your spiritual armor. This is a time for dubious and serious contemplation and wise choices, as without perseverance and foresight into the issues that stand before you, the outcome may prove hazardous for you in the end. Think of this warning as the spiritual essence of the fraudulent and dishonest Edward Kelly, who enchanted and beguiled the wise Dr. John Dee. There may be someone within your circle or just beyond it who covets something you have or perhaps even you as an object of monetary gain, property, or lust. Be ever cautious and wise in your decisions now. Although this may refer to a man or woman who desires what you have, it may also refer to an agency, a business, or a family that has a hidden agenda for you. The old adage "Patience is a virtue" is in full force for you now, so keep all your senses open.

Ʊ

Life Cycle, Natural Order, Cosmic Upheaval

ABU-MA'SHAR (C. 787–886 BC)

Abu-Ma'shar, also known as Albumazar, was the Arab astrólogos, seer, and author of such scholarly treatises as *Introductorium Astronomiam* and *De Magnis Conjunctionibus,* both of which represent the concepts of cycle and natural order in the context of the Theban Oracle. Although the majority of Abu-Ma'shar's research and contributions to the astrological arts did not reach European scholars until the 14th century, his works demonstrate the Aristotelian influence on both the sciences and occult philosophies. Moreover, it may be that

Abu-Ma'shar was partially responsible for the rebirth of such thinking in Western cultures.

Of his primary arena of thought, he proposed that there is a natural order to the stars that influences mankind and future events. And because the concept of astrology is based on the facts of natural order and cyclical realities within the universe, we may surmise that all things rise and fall, living and inert, and that all things are part of this process. Therefore, as all things within the heavens must operate as such, there must be a common thread of events that will "naturally" take place for us as well. Here too, in all our corporeal states there will be various stages of birth, death, and rebirth in one form or another. We must accept constant change within growth, as well as its decline and eventual death, following a spiritual transformation, where instead of true death, there is only a natural sequence.

With the fledgling lessons of Abu-Ma'shar we see that what is conceived as an ending is simply a continuation. As with the summer, soon shall come the winter, and with the winter, soon shall come the spring; never an ending, merely that which follows a natural cycle.

DIVINATORY MEANINGS

The *Abu-Ma'shar Theban Stone* relates that there must be a cyclic order for all things, literally translating that you are to expect a similar process and transformation soon. This example of this Theban stone focuses directly on self-change and transformation. It is an important stone because you are receiving silent signals now, which may go undetected if you are not vigilant in your thinking. Like the countless movements and cosmic conjunctions taking place in the heavens without our knowledge, here too your inner celestial workings may go unseen, so try to mentally and spiritually prepare yourself for the cyclical aspects of your being to change now.

The message here represents a divine gift. Where in the natural order and cycle, something in your life is indeed ending, let this natural event take place. With the acceptance and understanding of this comes sacred knowledge and blessings for you. Once you recognize that with life comes death, and with death comes life— renewed in one form or another—which is the key to bliss and wisdom, you will find an internal contentment. Accept transformation.

The *Abu-Ma'shar Theban Stone* counsels that there will be new encounters for you now, that new people may be entering your life, and that new situations and new opportunities will soon appear. You need to be acutely aware now, as this cycle may be as delicate as a newborn baby, who needs to be nurtured and loved with great care and responsibility. Now is a time to explore all aspects of life. It counsels for you to open yourself to this forthcoming experience, as there will be a source of fortune for you in the near future.

A STONE FACED IN REVERSE

If this stone is drawn faced away from you, it may indicate that though you are aware of the call for natural change and cyclic order, you may be avoiding its pull toward this predestined transformation. As many issues, situations, and places may act as safe harbors in our lives, it may be difficult to accept this pull for change. Regardless, it is time to drift away from that safe harbor and explore what lies outside the calm, seemingly protected waters of your inner world. Now is the time for trusting what is taking place within you and flow with where it sways you. Though you may feel like a leaf in the wind, unable to guide this unseen force, simply know that all will end right with you. The universe has a plan for you.

Although there may be a lack of understanding regarding what cycle and change is currently taking place for you now, making you feel somewhat overwhelmed, remember that like the stars moving in their orbits, you have no power to alter or change such passages, and that this change that is taking place in you now should not be delayed, as you cannot stop what must take place. You should not be dismayed as you enter this orbit of change; simply go with the flow. It will take you where you need to go. Trust in the direction the cosmic forces are sending you.

Discipline, Regulation, Self-Order, Divine Nourishment

JOHANNES TRITHEMIUS (C. 1462–1516)

Johannes Trithemius represents the elemental and philosophical realms of discipline and self-order. In spite of being born into poverty, he was able to prosper in all manners of education and understanding. As a boy, he had a profound love and inclination for all things scripted and lettered. While still a young man, he left his ancestral home in search of wisdom and spiritual enlightenment, crossing near and far to collect as much information on magick and related sciences as he could. During his journey, he was caught in a terrible thunderstorm and was temporarily forced to seek shelter within the Benedictine monastery of Saint Martin on Sponheim. When he was preparing to leave, however, the storm mysteriously returned, prompting him to believe this was an act of God and remain there. He eventually become a leading theologian and later earned the position of Abbott of Sponheim. He was considered a force of wisdom and an authority on the occult, and was loved by all who knew him.

Trithemius authored many books on various forms of writing and cryptography, and it was he who introduced the Theban script as an angelic alphabet of great significance, which he proposed in his most respected tomes, *Polygraphia* and the *Steganographia*. Undeniably, Cornelius Agrippa, his cherished student, then borrowed the Theban alphabet for his *De Occulta Philosophia*. Regardless of hardships and the need for self-sacrifice, Johannes Trithemius was able to prosper during his life, and was revered as a key inspiration to many others in search of wisdom. Through the intense discipline and precise order with which he led his daily life, he proves to be the quintessential icon of order and divine regulation in the context of the Theban Oracle.

DIVINATORY MEANINGS

The *Johannes Trithemius Theban Stone* represents the process of order and the need for cyclical regimens. It also translates as "anything which is sacrificed in one area, must also be favorably replenished elsewhere, in one form or another." Simply said, when one relinquishes the old and outdated habits that have grown with us over the many years, we replace them with new and hopefully wiser habits, which will culminate in better lifestyles and future outcomes. This Theban stone denotes a fertile mind that promotes personal growth and advancement, both symbolically and in actuality.

This stone promises growth in the higher aspects of learning and related matters, including but not limited to school, home, and business matters, as well as within the spiritual and emotional realms. This stone also suggests that there is something leading you to some form of success within the aforementioned areas, and that you will recognize them when such issues arise. This is a time for blossoming and taking on divine nourishment.

In order to achieve what this stone foretells, you must first separate from your natural resistance to change and from being overly proud. As with the goodly Abbott of Sponheim, you too must relinquish old and outdated concepts and accept the wisdom that is heading your way. To do this you must form a somewhat rigid plan of self-order. You must first embrace a logical yet common disciplinary regimen in order to accomplish this. There is no question here; it is do, or do not, there can be no in-between. It is time to be steadfast and to adopt a positive attitude and move forward, simply leaving the old and outdated behind you. There is no need to look back.

A STONE FACED IN REVERSE

Receiving this stone faced away from you predicts a simple issue, that there is a lack of self-discipline in one form or another within your life. Everyone living on this earth will lack discipline from time to time; whether forming a stable and working lifestyle for ourselves or knowing when not to have that extra dessert after a meal, we will always be wanting in some way. We are humans, after all, and mistakes are what separate us from the Almighty in the heavens and the many angels, who are without flaw. Yet our humanity also empowers us to find success regardless of our station during our corporeal state. There is hope!

This oracle reflects that it is time to sit down awhile and seriously reflect on your character and present status. What is interfering with your growth and life process now? Are you making the right choices and actions? Now may be the time to do some serious investigating in order to identify just what blocks you from sincere and purposeful growth. Indeed, once you apply the right amount of discipline in your daily regimens, whether it is in school, at the office, or at home, creating a working plan of self-order and control over the frivolous, you will be assured of advancing in all areas of your life. Now is the time to think seriously on your life path. Is there a proper level of order and self-discipline in the structure of your life?

Ϥ

Stagnation, Languishing, Persecution, Surrender

DR. SIMON FORMAN (1552–1611)

Dr. Simon Forman, the Elizabethan practitioner of alternative medicine, occultist, and mystic, serves as the example of *stagnation, persecution,* and *languishing* in the context of the Theban Oracle. This physician and surgeon, mostly thought of as a charlatan and menace, should also be remembered as one of the first to apply unique combinations of physic and magick to his nontraditional treatments. Though his experiments with herbs and healing waters had ushered in a rare and esoteric understanding for the wise and commoner alike, his endeavors nonetheless aroused suspicions and resentful feelings from his contemporaries. Such altered his already tainted reputation and hindered his exaltation in medicine and the science of magick.

By the late 16th century, when the plague gripped London, Simon Forman remained to help the sick, while the doctors who condemned him fled for personal safety. This act of bravery, along with saving many lives, including his own as result of his alternative medicines, would forever place his image in the light of good, in spite of the many insults he endured from his detractors. Although some would believe Dr. Forman to be unsuitable to exercise the arts of medicine and healing, being considered a heretic for applying astrology and magick within his medical practice, and for help-ing the sick on the Sabbath day, he would be forced to endure the hurtful slander from his peers throughout his kindly occupation. Thankfully, his heroics during the four-year plague had assured the grateful that most of his intentions were good in nature, and that he was indeed a just and caring physician.

Throughout his professional career Dr. Forman would be the victim of many accusations and crimes, serving time in prison for his occult practices and for prescribing what were then considered to be dangerous potions to treat ailments, resulting in being banned from practicing medicine by a council of his peers. Indeed, though he was constantly hounded by those jealous of his deeds and mis-trustful of his herbal experimentations, Dr. Forman, though a good man, had to suffer the stagnation of stunted mentalities and languish through waves of hate and persecution. Through all this, however, he rose above the small-mindedness and the contempt of his peers and continued to aid those in need.

DIVINATORY MEANINGS

The idea of stagnation and languishing sounds terrible; however, the magickal reasoning of each word translates more toward hibernation and psychic storage than that of doom and gloom. This is actually a time for temporary submission instead of action. The negative connotation of this aspect of the Theban example may translate to a spiritual winter, where there is a temporary hindrance to growth. Now is the time for restraint and learning instead of skirmish or conflict. Like Dr. Forman, you may be involved in a situation in which accusations and implications exist. This may be a time when you feel the most vulnerable and powerless. This is acceptable now, as fighting what faces you will only hold you back, while your peers and contemporaries advance. This is not a time to compete with those who would see you fail in your good endeavors. Stand tall now, but think before you act.

Now is the time to show patience and to continue on your current path. Sadly, there are those who choose to savor another's torment, whose low self-esteem demands some form of compensation for the achievements of their resented victims. Remember the path Dr. Forman took in his professional life. It may have been turbulent and unwise due to some of his choices, but it was his reverence for the health and life of others that made him stand out among his peers, not the negative hearsay that his detractors had created about him.

This is a time of hibernation and self-contemplation. A cycle of development must occur before you advance in any direction. As such cycles must take place before birth or rebirth, now is your time to concentrate on the behavior of others and to inwardly surmise the possible motives and wishes others may have for you without becoming mistrustful. This is a time for deep and soulfully pensive thought. If you're living a good and honest life, then simply stay on course. Though uncouth and envious people may seemingly advance ahead of you, in the end, you will win the race with a clear conscience.

A STONE FACED IN REVERSE

If you have drawn this stone faced away from you, it may signify that you have been giving in to the small-mindedness of those around you. Perhaps you have been playing the fool, which at times may appear fanciful and amusing for friends or acquaintances but leaves you feeling empty after the laughter ends. Perhaps you're experiencing a drain on your energies, which you may be associating with the attachment of someone who appears close to you. Be cautious now, as you may be the victim of psychic draining or another's ill will.

This Theban stone is putting you on alert now. Now is a time to look into the reasoning behind all friendships and acquaintanceships and to analyze motives and goals of those around you. Is this relationship for you, or are you simply a catalyst for another's progress? Now is the time to pull back and spiritually hibernate for a time; to become mindful of your situation and placement within your social setting. Whether at work or when at home, it's best to thoroughly examine the motives, passions, and goals of those around you. The need for deep mindfulness is in full force now.

ෆ

Rage, Negative Temperament, Ending of Innocence

GILLES DE RAIS (1404–1440)

Likely to be remembered as one of the most notoriously evil men of the Medieval age, the once honored and proud knight, *Gilles de Rais*, would fall into the realm of black magick and disgrace. Though serving alongside Joan of Arc in many campaigns, and being described as nothing less than a true godly man, assumed by all to be a proud and devout Christian—who was not only brave and skillful in combat, but was also a Marshal of France, a scholar and soldier, and even a patron of the arts—he harbored a terrible secret. Though Gilles de Rais was initially loved and respected by all who knew him, having an almost saintly demeanor, a terrible dark side to this man was to be discovered, a secret that would instigate the call for revenge and echo the rage of the French people that would be heard across the oceans of time.

Accused of murdering at least one hundred and forty children in the name of wealth, power, and perverted lust, Gilles de Rais would finally confess to the heinous crimes of the murder of innocents. He squandered his fortunes, and many historians believe that he delved in the black arts in order to gain favor from dark forces and like minions, in order to rebuild his treasury and illustrious status. And, though he claimed not to have worshiped the devil, there was nonetheless evidence to condemn the baron to death.

One may wish to consider this the "death stone," in the context of the Theban Oracle, should there be a similarity to the Tarot. Although this stone may in one way relate to the many crimes of the bloody baron, it does so only in the representation that an ending is approaching and that the naïve aspects of innocence will soon wane. This is a natural part of the life cycle. This Theban stone relates the natural movements that reverberate within all regions of our lives. It is a natural representation of the shadowy aspects of our nature.

DIVINATORY MEANINGS

As with all things in life, there is an eventual ending to what is. In life, there being rage and anger, negativity and loss of innocence, these things, although painful and difficult to bear at times, will almost always wane and depart us. Although the iconological persona of this Theban stone may appear to be the most degrading and heart-wrenching, in actuality, it holds within it the many changes that come about within the reality of life. The attributes of the *Gilles de Rais Theban Stone* signify that there is indeed a monumental change on the way, change that will in fact offer a sense of divine understanding, which will result in freedom from certain habits and emotional ties, eventually culminating in spiritual growth.

The liberation of worn and obsolete things is attributed to this stone and indicates an urgent need within the psyche to break free from small thinking now and to turn away from material riches, which may be the primal reality in your existence. Instead, enlist the experience of unconventional emotions and listen to what is being said from within. Much like the terrible secret Gilles de Rais held for so many years, it was only a matter of time until his actions and belief systems would conclude with the fruits of his wicked labors. And, though our secrets are far less in severity, we too must continue to grow by loss and by the death of our habits and negative patterns. Only when we allow this natural function to discharge and wane away will we come closer to divine understanding and enlightenment.

A Stone Faced in Reverse

Receiving this stone faced away should alert you that a seemingly drastic change is about to occur in your life, and that you may incur substantial loss or damage in the process. Whether you experience your plans going amiss, or a romantic relationship fails, it is important to embrace what losses may occur in order to grow, essentially being encouraged to appreciate and accept what transpires in your life. This is the spice of the human condition and is the needed medicine for you right now.

This arrangement of the *Gilles de Rais Theban Stone* may also indicate that there is indeed a foreboding aspect to your nature that must be addressed at all costs. Whether it is one of rage and anger or simply having a negative outlook or demeanor toward your life or yourself, you must let this portion of yourself die and commit to a total departure from such beliefs and thinking. Now is the time to feel that you are a blank canvas, able to have painted a new picture or outlook the way you want it to be. Remember, the more severe your issues are, the more there is a need for change in your life, as such change is required in order to advance to the next stage of your corporeal understanding. Take this stone as your wake-up call to better things. Though it is an early morning wake-up call, try to rouse yourself awake enough to get the message. The message here is distinct and very personal for you, where only you will comprehend the inner meanings that are showing themselves in relation to this oracle. Listen and be true to yourself.

♍

Willpower, a Crusade, a Priceless Gift

DR. NICHOLAS FLAMEL (C. 1330–1417)

The many aspects and particulars of great willpower and the divine crusade are well defined in this 14th-century alchemist, scribe, and beloved bibliophile. *Dr. Nicholas Flamel,* the loved Parisian medical doctor, known for his devotion to ancient tomes and the written word, had extraordinary acquisitions of rare manuscripts and religious scrolls. Dr. Flamel's scholarly pursuits led him to various understandings of esoteric wisdom, becoming an authority on the occult, and enjoying instructing commoner and nobleman alike.

As Flamel's understanding of the magickal arts grew, so did his authority as an astrologer and provost of the divinatory arts, where legend tells us that Dr. Flamel was visited by an angel in a life-altering vision—a vision that would lend great and powerful instructions to compose an illustrious book. This angel is said to have presented the good doctor a book made of a golden metal and coarse tree bark. This mystical book had only twenty-one pages within it, and three enigmatic drawings heading each chapter of seven pages. The angel instructed that Dr. Flamel would one day have this sacred tome, but it must remain unintelligible until a special time when he would discern all its pages, where none other would see or understand. Indeed, this cryptic vision and angelic message remained with him for many years, and fueled his interest and scholarly investigations into alchemy and the hermetic arts, to become one of Europe's most venerated authorities in the metaphysical sciences. With his own laboratory, Nicolas Flamel and his devoted wife Pernella set out to pursue the Philosopher's Stone and a grand potion known as the *elixir vitae.*

Around 1357, Dr. Flamel encountered a strange, foreign scholar in need of money, who was selling an odd book made of copper and wood. Intrigued, Flamel bought the strange tome, with the mysterious traveling scholar then departing as quickly as he had arrived. Upon further inspection of this curious acquisition, he became astounded to find that it was the very same book the angel showed him years before. This strange and seemingly ancient tome had Latin text inscribed on it. It contained twenty-one leaves, and had many cryptic hieroglyphs painted about it. Each seventh page of the book was emblazoned with beautiful yet anomalous ciphers and artwork. Although a complete translation of this book escaped the virtuous doctor, his love and devotion to understand its strange purpose personified his divine crusade for goodness and love to all mankind.

Though extremely wealthy and popular, Dr. Flamel and his family lived a humble, pious life, almost without luxury. Indeed, they spent most of their fortune on charities for the poor and sick, having constructed fourteen hospitals and three chapels, as well as funding many humanitarian organizations to assist the poor and aid the churches. This husband and wife team, known for their great intellect and compassionate efforts, understood that the abandonment of earthly pleasures for the well-being of their fellow man, woman, and child was the highest and noblest of human qualities.

DIVINATORY MEANINGS

The *Dr. Nicholas Flamel Theban Stone* represents the highest order of human compassion and soul. It regards the divine crusade, which serves all and rewards the faithful in turn. This Theban stone exemplifies that many beneficial rewards will occur when offering simple love and compassion to others; be it an offering of wealth or of brotherly or sisterly love, it applies to the righteous endeavor that you are committed to. Receiving this stone persuades you to embark on the gentle crusade of goodness. If this is your demeanor to begin with, it therefore encourages you to stay on that course, continuing with what you are doing. You should not count on instant results, however, as inner patience is urgently needed now.

This Theban example represents the power of will and the need for progression. Nicholas Flamel, who found the benefits of higher learning and all things mystical, understood that in order to succeed in his pursuits, he must use every aspect of his willpower to continue with what he had begun. Here too, you are advised to continue with whatever element of willpower has a hold on you. If working with people, whether it is with children or adults, this Theban stone counsels that you give as much as you possibly can. Your gift to another should be of the heart, as this is beyond all the silver and gold in the world.

The farmer who respects and loves the land, and who gives freely of what is needed to bring in the season's harvest, must prepare the soil and sow the seed, but he must also care for the land as it prepares for its yield. To do this, he must offer time, sacrifice, and hard work daily in order to enjoy the fruits of his labor. Here too, like the mother to be, you must rightfully contribute, fortify, feed, and love so that the baby to be born is healthy and strong. And, as any mother knows, such sacrifices and compassion don't end when she bears her child. In our daily life, this too applies. Remember to be mindful that perseverance along with patience is essential for any crusade. Without it, your efforts will be in vain.

A STONE FACED IN REVERSE

If this Theban stone is drawn faced away from you, it may indicate a lack of compassion in a vital area of your being. That is to say that your attention toward things regarding the love of yourself and others may be lacking. Perhaps you have done this in the past and feel you have been punished for your efforts. Perhaps you have withdrawn from the crusade you were once on, as the pain was far too much for you to bear. This may be the time to join the fight once again; to return to the path that once brought you happiness; to reopen that conduit where joy once flowed in your life. It may be time to rejoin the human race, not only for your own benefit, but for the benefit of those special people in your life.

This reversed stone may also signify that you are becoming aggravated by something in your life. Whether related to love or work, there appears to be a hindrance to the process. Are you giving all of yourself, or is your offering merely for the conveyance of perceived goals and emotions to others? Perhaps you are overwhelmed now, overcome with negative thoughts toward others or even yourself. Now is the time to put these barriers aside and reflect on them, understanding that what you see before you can be changed, no matter how painful those issues are. Though Nicolas Flamel could have easily taken his wealth for himself only, he chose the compassionate route, not for fortune or glory but because he knew it was the right thing to do. Like this loving alchemist, you may show equal empathy and respect, not necessarily by giving material riches, but with the far more precious element that costs nothing: compassion.

♏

Divine Understanding, Angelic Overseeing, Transitional Harmony

WILLIAM LILLY (1602–1681)

One of England's most influential astrologers of the 17th century, *William Lilly* was titled the Merlin of his day. Lilly's astrological almanacs and prophetic booklets had remarkable effects on the public of his day. So much so that military generals, heads of state, and nobility came to William Lilly to be advised, making him a legend in his own time.

Having lived in an age when most believed that astrological movements had a direct influence on human affairs and cultural events, Lilly was able to survive the English Civil Wars, faring well throughout the rule of King Charles I and even surviving the religious vehemence of Cromwell's reign of parliamentary rule, right on until the Restoration and the return of the royalists and King Charles II. Indeed, Lilly created for himself the title of the foremost astrologer in England, but was also able to apply the proper zeal of accepted religious ideals to his metaphysical setting.

His published works included psychic interpretations and predictions—such as the return of the plague, and the great fire of London in 1666—as well as many astrological almanacs, including his famous treatise on Christian astrology. In the end, William Lilly had secured for himself the title of benefactor and patron of both the Christian faith and the enigmatic realms of horary astrology—unquestionably an enormous feat for that age, if not any.

Because Lilly was able to relate the heavenly realms of the most in-depth forms of astrology with the often violent nature of the Christian faith, without denying or betraying the two very separate doctrines, this luminary is positioned within the realms of divine understanding and insight, and serves as the key aspect of transitional harmony between opposing forces and the nature of angelic intervention.

DIVINATORY MEANINGS

The *William Lilly Theban Stone* represents the very nature of transitional harmony. This stone expresses the transitory nature of the spirit and emotional self and implies that various shifts are taking place now. In effect, this Theban example foretells that there is a good adjustment in store for you now. Whether this refers to a physical change or that of a spiritual and emotional nature, the overall quality of this adjustment remains to be seen. This may represent that something new is about to take place. Perhaps this refers to an adjustment in attitude or opinion, or that there will be a change in a life situation, such as in love and romance. Either way, expect to witness a metamorphosis, either grand or diminutive, soon.

This Theban stone exemplifies that there will be an improvement in a present situation; that a steady development is occurring now, so sit back and prepare for something good to happen. Like the growth of the body or the mind, nothing happens all at once. As such, you can always expect many frequent shifts and changes throughout your being, so be patient, as miracles often work at various speeds. This is a time for rejoicing in the gift of adjustment, which will produce only positive things for you now. Accept this well-earned gift with an air of reverence and humility, allowing for the goodly aspects of your fate to occur without delay. Let the sun shine on you now, for in the end, blessings will indeed shine happily on you.

To ensure that this cosmic gift finds you well, be prepared to share in your delights with those not feeling as happy as they could. Doing so will add to the positive dividends of your spiritual bank account, as the more you give, the more interest you will collect. Therefore, the more joy you share, the more you will have saved for yourself on a rainy day.

A STONE FACED IN REVERSE

When the *William Lilly Theban Stone* is drawn in reverse, it implies that there is stagnation within the natural transitions of your being. Basically said, the natural movements that formulate a healthy and happy lifestyle appear to be blocked. When this stone is faced away, it signifies that you might be out of phase right now, meaning that you must try to recognize what is missing in your thinking and habits now. For instance, the student who fails to graduate from a difficult class will have to re-examine and devote more time to that subject. He cannot speed up this process or advance without doing so.

Like this hypothetical student, you too must re-examine the issues at hand before you proceed. Patience and devotion are called for, as there can be no other method. Understand that receiving this stone reversed need not be a bad thing. It may merely express that the opportunity is not yet precisely for you; that the joys that are rightfully yours will come to you when the time is right. Simply continue in a steady and determined path in order to achieve progress. Patience and steadfastness are in order now.

A Sacrifice, Solitude, the Sacred Quest

PARACELSUS (1493–1541)

Paracelsus was born Auroleus Phillipus Theostratus Bombastus von Hohenheim, the son of a well-known physician and Grand Master of a Teutonic Order. "Paracelsus" was taken from the word "para" meaning above or beyond, and "Celsus" to honor the 1st-century Roman physician. This luminary is remembered as the essential icon of the practices of medicine and high alchemy.

At the age of sixteen, Paracelsus began his formal education at the University of Basel, where he studied alchemy, surgery, and medicine. By adulthood, he had become known as the precursor of modern chemical pharmacology and therapeutics, and as the most original medical thinker of his century. The Abbot Johannes Trithemius, the adroit instructor and mentor of Cornelius Agrippa, was largely responsible for Paracelsus's alchemical interests, advising him to learn from the masters from around the world. And so the young Paracelsus traveled throughout Germany, France, Hungary, the Netherlands, Denmark, Sweden, and Russia in search of wisdom. The fledgling student considered wisdom a sacred quest, and such did he find. Indeed, by the time he was in his early thirties, he had been an army surgeon, a respectable doctor, a noted magus, a university professor, and an innovator of new medicines and techniques. He was, without a doubt, a true master of the sciences and metaphysics.

As time progressed, Paracelsus became very bold and even overzealous in temperament and action, to the point that he made many a foe. By denouncing the revered works of Galen and the standard practice of medicine as a whole, as well as the teachings of his own university, he become so unalterable in nature that school officials and other authorities would come to consider him a heretic and a despot. In the end, Paracelsus was slain as a result of his overly bold and overzealous nature. Though the details of his demise remain a mystery, his end may certainly prove a testament to the danger of having too much pride and arrogance.

DIVINATORY MEANINGS

The *Paracelsus Theban Stone* represents the need for a new beginning within one's thinking and life. An honest willingness to change internally is required now, for having a true relationship to one-self is of primary importance. The mantra here is to become and remain modest and true to oneself rather than being overzealous and overly proud. This Theban stone offers the simple advice that no matter how wise you are or how great your significance, it is important to remain still on this occasion, surrendering the needs of outward recognition instead of yielding to the temptations of pride and arrogance.

There are times when one needs to seek out credit for one's deeds and accomplishments, as this is healthy for a working self-esteem, but it is also important not to over-focus on one's accomplishments, as this not only takes away from one's own credibility but also contributes to the ill feelings and the abhorrence of others. Rather, remaining content in your deeds alone is the answer here, whereby adding a sense of modesty and nobility to your persona will only add to your overall character.

While it is always wise to remain receptive to the needs and impulses of self-recognition, and even fame to some extent, remember the flaws of the wise Paracelsus, who with all his learning and wisdom fell short in the eyes of his peers and enemies, thus prematurely ending his beneficial offerings and even his life. Although your situation may not be as life threatening, the same image may be forming to a hidden adversary within your circle.

Now is the time to seriously reflect on yourself, your self-image as it may be perceived by others around you, and retreat to an inner solitude, just as many great minds often do. Here, you will begin to see your actions and images; for even when congenial and outgoing as you can be, you might nonetheless be tendering sour grapes to those near you. A time of reflection, silence and solitude is in order here.

A STONE FACED IN REVERSE

If the *Paracelsus Theban Stone* is faced away from you, it may signify that you are mishandling your ego and self-importance. Perhaps this remains within the arena of only one issue, or within a series of such issues. In either case, a blockage exists. This is the time to look into yourself as clearly and deeply as you can, denying any attempt to hide anything from yourself, as doing so will only magnify such blockages and end with unfavorable results.

This Theban stone advises you to look within, in essence, to perform a self-diagnostic exam, exploring all the details for any abnormalities. Whether there are issues stemming from your past, by way of unfortunate happenings, or unresolved pain, it is vital to take a good hard look. Once done, and the issues recognized, it is time to itemize, catalog, and then systematically isolate and quarantine any negative issues. Because this is an emotional and spiritual releasing, a sacrifice of the old ways is called for. Solitude for contemplation is needed more than ever. Now is a good time to take a long walk through the woods or on a deserted beach to contemplate internal issues and situations. Consider everything and be honest with yourself. Afterward, you should be able to look at yourself with a scientific kind of honesty and defeat what issues may be. Now is the time to think with patience and tenacity.

9

Endurance, Steadfastness, Rectification, Balance

CORNELIUS AGRIPPA (1486–1535)

The persona essence of *Cornelius Agrippa* represents *endurance* and *steadfastness*, and is considered a patriarch of true angelic magick among modern metaphysical scholars today. He is also seen by most students of the occult arts and sciences as the innovator of the scholarly investigation into the astrological realms, even though this intriguing individual had to overcome the many detractors and naysayers of his day. As a soldier, ambassador, physician, university lecturer, and he who was knighted by Emperor Maximilian, Heinrich Cornelius Agrippa von Nettesheim serves as the quintessential hierarchy of history's most respected and accomplished magi.

Agrippa's treatises, *De nobilitiate et praecelentia foemini sexus*—which describes his controversial beliefs regarding the nobility of the female sex—and his literary work *De incertitudine & vanitate scientiarum & artium*—which explores man's vanity and ambiguity of the sciences and arts—and of course his magnum opus, *De occulta philosophia*—which serves as one of the most scholarly examples of applied magick and Medieval metaphysics in history—remain the tour de force behind all modern works of occult practices. Having instituted the concepts of celestial cipher writing such as the Theban alphabet, and being a devoted advocate of Enochian and astrological magick, Agrippa has proven the art of scholarly endurance and steadfast effort with honor and pride. Indeed, his time-honored tomes exemplify the classical Neoplatonic, Hermetic, and Kabbalistic philosophies as related to Judaism, Christianity, and high magick, and have proven to be the singular, systematic demonstration of secret wisdoms as employed throughout Medieval and Renaissance Europe.

Agrippa's research into the magickal aspects of all things—whether of nature; the divination process; the significance of numerology and astrology; the power of talismans; the comprehension of elementary, celestial, and intellectual realities; or the divine aspects and representations of the angelic and daemonic orders, all which had paved the way we understand magick today—was not always well received by his peers. If truth be told, Agrippa was seen by many as not only a heretic but knowingly in league with devils and daemons for his beliefs and practices. His faith for seeking the truth and for his steadfast nature angered his contemporaries, regardless of his associations with popes and kings.

In his day, Agrippa had been loved and cherished by many a scholar and nobleman alike, enlightening and inspiring such notable magi and wizards as Paraclesus, Johannes Trithemius, and Nostradamus. Yet, even with such honored brethren, he had to endure the attacks of those who lacked vision and spiritual forbearance. Because this wise scholar was able to tolerate the small-mindedness of his detractors and move beyond the aggression of his oppressors, we are able to see his prudent intentions today. For these reasons, and for having the internal fortitude of spirit and scholarly demeanor to avoid conflicts, and for remaining steadfast in times of opposition and religious upheaval, we devote this icon in the context of the Theban Oracle.

DIVINATORY MEANINGS

The *Cornelius Agrippa Theban Stone* calls for the conscious constraint of mind, body, and spirit. Though this oracle expresses an understanding of one's entitlement to verbal and spiritual expression, and of tenacity in obtaining one's personal achievements, you are informed to be cautious now. The necessity of such restraint refers not to your achievement and overall accomplishment, but to your outward pride and self-esteem, which might be attracting negative attention from opposition and colleague alike. Remember Agrippa's plight because of those who were suspicious or jealous of his achievements and honors. This proved to be his constant nemesis. Instead of retaliation and fueling further reprisals, choose the better part of valor, and keep to your small order of benefactors, constraining your true wisdom away from those lacking in vision and respect.

This Theban Oracle represents the need to pull away from those who, although confessing their support, may in the darker recesses of their psyche hold a grudge against your success. This may not flow from a negative place of ill will or abhorrence on their part as much as it does from a lack of self-esteem. This person or group of people may simply desire the recognition you now appreciate. Although the positive aspects of your demeanor and routine may represent only good, it is time to understand the negative aspects of those around you—not to judge or condemn, but to learn and adjust for the better.

Rely on the simple answer now, and choose the humble path over that of the glare of confrontation. Doing so will hush the intemperate souls, those who are not on the same spiritual path as you, and those who cannot celebrate your gains. Do not take the naysayer and spiritual aggressor personally as you will not force a change by doing so. In essence, this Theban stone is telling you to not be overly proud. Simply give thanks for the favorable aspects of your life, whether business achievements or family or romantic bliss. Smile softly and offer the hand of peace, even to your most notable adversary or detractor. Doing so will only cast you in the most high of places, where you will shine in golden reverence.

A Stone Faced in Reverse

Receiving the *Cornelius Agrippa Theban Stone* faced away may be showing you that a healthy transformation in the form of modesty and humbleness is needed now. In addition, the limitation of harsh ego and the fostering of good public relations may be called for, as over-pride and too much zeal, though appreciated or overlooked by some, may be annoying and chastising to others. When this stone is drawn in this position, you are put on notice that the feelings of others are in question now. It may refer to one's anger, displeasure, or mistrust.

Not having the restraint to deal with a situation in an honest and humble manner will only result in further aggressions, be it in the workplace or the home. Step back now and think of another's feelings. Be sure to analyze the situation at hand and look deeply into the hearts of those around you. In short, offer the wealth of silence instead of self-approval or too much praise, and give thanks instead of expecting it. Doing so will calm the rough seas of human emotions, and make the agitated sharks in those waters swim in the other direction.

Interference, Disturbance, Submission, Withdrawal

ROBERT FLUDD (1574–1637)

Robert Fludd, literally a Renaissance man of his day, was well respected as an alchemist, scientist, philosopher, astrologer, and musician, as well as a respected authority on the Kabbalah. Oxford educated, and a man of letters, he made his living as a physician in London and was considered to be one of the premier English healer-philosophers of the 17th century. He was influenced primarily by the doctrines of the Swiss physician and alchemist Paracelsus, applying many of his medicinal and alchemical speculations to the newer concepts within his century's realm of science and magick. It was Robert Fludd's theory that the spiritual and physical realities within the universe were identical in purpose and reasoning, believing that God was at the center of all such works and doctrines, meaning simply that all things under the stars were of God's influences, where the concepts of good and evil were naturally intertwined.

Robert Fludd was unique in that he adapted the Eastern concept of the *Yin* and *Yang* to that of common Western thought. He believed that dualism existed within the nature of all things—man, plants and animals, and the heavens—trusting that both light and darkness could exist in one circumference together. In the realms of good and evil, he believed that there was a natural inclination, which flowed in all directions; whether toward good or evil, there was a natural purpose for such responses. And, because he felt that this natural matrix was inherent in all things, he applied such philosophies to his works in alchemy and high magick.

As a devout member of the fledgling Rosicrucian order, he brought many new ideals and theories to the public, writing several theosophical manuscripts highlighting such theories. Fludd's scholarly works—*Utriusque Cosmi, Maioris Scilicet et Minoris, Metaphysica, Physica atque Technica Historia,* and *De Philosophia Moysaica*—brought about a studious transformation toward the practical and scientific aspects of magick, including the art of divination. Indeed, because

Robert Fludd was capable of visually and spiritually distinguishing the natural aspects of both the good and evil that reside within us and within all things, he represents the significant modalities of *disturbance* and *interference*, as well as *submission* and *withdrawal*, as being integral components in the human condition.

DIVINATORY MEANINGS

When the *Robert Fludd Theban Stone* is drawn, it reflects the separation of one aspect from another, or the mingling of two separate aspects within a grander circumference. These "aspects" can signify many things in our lives, from business affairs to matters of the heart, and all in between. This Theban stone's representations show us a rather dark and foreboding answer at first, yet once we look closer, we will see that there is a ray of light shining through that darkness. If this stone is drawn in the context of a complex question, again, take the time to concentrate on what this could mean to you, as it will tend to point to one significant aspect of your life.

Primarily, this Theban stone revolves around a series of issues that may be pressing you to take a particular action that you may be avoiding. This action might refer to a relationship that is harmful, debasing, or simply unfruitful. Perhaps this stone refers to a place of status, which may have become a heavy burden over time, where before it was beneficial and pleasant. This oracle may be showing you that this is the time to separate from the old and unhappy paths you've been traveling on during your life—to look above and beyond your situation for that one answer that will make a positive difference for you. This stone may be asking you to seriously deliberate whether or not you should consider withdrawing from a current situation that stands before you.

If this advice is worthy for you to take, then simply consider the outcome that you withdraw from. After all, are the things we hang on to a tangible reality or a perceived status symbol in our lives? Remember, because the answer lies within you, and only within you, you must take heed of all the elements in and around your life's circumference, remembering not to let any issue go unturned. If you ignore one aspect of your situation, you will simply be denying its existence. Like the wise alchemist Robert Fludd, study both the lit and the darkened regions of your soul, as what peers at you from that supposed light may in truth be far more frightening than what peers at you from the darkness.

A Stone Faced in Reverse

When the *Robert Fludd Theban Stone* is drawn faced away from you, it may be suggesting that you are holding on to deep-rooted ideals and outdated philosophies. As doing so falls within the time-honored traditions of human classical conditioning, which is simply a side effect of being human, there is no need for regret or shame now. Though turning away from these natural realities may be difficult, it is vital to press forward and make positive change regardless of the struggle it may require.

This stone calls for a radical departure from old traditions; look inward with complete honesty and clarity, and then choose wisely the course you must take. If you choose not to comply with the necessary changes that are gently calling for you at this time, to surrender or withdraw from what is emotionally or spiritually ailing you, then this tradition, no matter how degrading and painful, will sadly continue. In short, you must first identify the *interference* that is taking place in your life's situation now, and then recognize the dangers of the *disturbance* it is creating. Second, you must treat this situation with the appropriate measures in order to move on with your life. If, for instance, this oracle is telling you to end a hurtful relationship, or choose not to continue a harmful business venture, then you must follow your instincts: Trust in yourself.

ȣ

Wealth, a Tribute, a Spiritual Path, the Unseen

GIORDANO BRUNO (1548–1600)

The Theban symbol that best describes the divine gift of living for knowledge, and the refusal of ignorance over truth, is personified by the kindly philosophical monk, *Giordano Bruno*. This Italian philosopher, Dominican priest, and translator of high magick should be remembered as one of the most potent thinkers of the Renaissance age. His research into new thinking may have sealed his fate among the hate-filled and unsophisticated, yet he continues to open new avenues of critical thinking to this day.

Bruno was also one of the first to research and lecture on the scientific ramifications of memory and thought processes. In 1582, he applied his scholarly findings, which he referred to as *Ars Memoria* ("The Art of Memory"), to a major treatise, highlighting the concept of what is now considered the classic technique of mnemonic coding. In addition, Bruno used this and similar methods of placing icons and visual images to memory-enhancing techniques, which had excellent results. Having an interest in the mystic, he applied these concepts to the art of magick, again, taking the center stage for invention and foresight.

Bruno published many scholarly works on thought magick—including *Cena de le Ceneri, Spaccio della Bestia transfinite,* and *De l'Infinito, Universo e Mondi*—all of which imply infinite reasoning and spirit to his many ideals. Though most of his works were directly related to the Dominican doctrine of Christianity, he also embraced more arcane topics, such as heliocentric astronomy as related by the works of Copernicus and the edicts of Egyptian Hermeticism, both which were seen as major profanations in his day. Indeed, with such an interest in metaphysics and the occult, it was just a matter of time until he would enrage the Church and the mighty pope. And though he was a devote priest and a man of faith, he was outspoken and direct in his opinion, which was of course a dangerous attribute to have in his day.

By the dawn of a new century, as he was arriving in Venice to continue his research, he was arrested by the pope's soldiers, the enforcers of the inquisition. After being imprisoned and tortured, he was forced to recant his views but soon abjured that declaration, which sent him to burn on the pyres of the sinful. As the crowds gathered, and a huge crucifix was forced to his face for him to plea for God's mercy, he is said to have pushed the icon away in defiance, saying he would rather die for truth than hate and lies. Certainly, in regard to his conviction that religion of his day was incorrect in its views and actions, his death would entice others to consider the contrary. Because of Giordano Bruno's contribution to scholarly thought and soul, this Theban stone reflects a divine tribute to all those who would refuse to sit still while oppression reigned.

DIVINATORY MEANINGS

The *Giordano Bruno Theban Stone* is an important stone, in that it reflects major self-renovations within the natural cycle of change. In a way, this is one of the most intriguing Theban stones, largely because it "shadows" your spiritual path identically in appearance and demeanor as your physical path. Yet because this spirit path for the most part remains hidden beneath the skin of the spiritual self and the ego, you will have to look deeper within yourself for the answers you need. Because understanding where this shadowy, misty pathway will guide you may prove too difficult while on your journey, it is going to take considerable effort on your part.

This Theban stone represents the divine gift of wealth. Not in the sense of riches or power, but that the self-transformation that is taking place within you now is a powerful transformation that will augment the emotional and spiritual aspects of the self. Now is the time to take an unexpected adventure, but the spiritual path you're now treading on will require a good amount of will and determination on your part. Do not stop as your resolve is vital: Keep pressing onward.

Much like the wise Giordano Bruno, the truth is becoming clear to you now, as the things you once took for truth and good are taking on a different light with your new vision. In your life, this may refer to several things, be it your faith, your philosophies, or your general outlook. Either way, you will be taking a road less traveled and will be encountering new and amazing things along the way. Be mindful to stay on that path, no matter what. Although you may witness suspicion, competition, and disapproval, simply stay on course. In the end, you will reach the goal you were always meant to reach, but in order to do this you must stay focused and always look from within.

A STONE FACED IN REVERSE

Receiving the *Giordano Bruno Theban Stone* faced away from you indicates that though you are indeed on the right path now, and that signs of triumph and affluence are happily appearing to you, you should be especially mindful of the dangers that may still be present. Understanding that a particularly dark time is behind you now and that significant things will now occur for you, be ever heedful of your past problems, failures, and losses in order not to repeat them.

This oracle respectfully advises that you not get too ahead of yourself, nor allow yourself to fall off the spiritual path by giving in to the earthly whims that often arise when joy sings out or when the laughter and wine flows in good company. Although you have seen the wolfish behavior of those who would profit by your loss and pain, try to embrace your good judgment and trust your gut feelings. Be content with your winnings, but be wise not to overspend them. In short, the more of this spiritual manna that you store away, the more you will have for a spiritually empty time. Stay cool in every aspect of your demeanor and action now, and accept this self-transformation and cosmic wealth in a stoic and wise manner.

♍

Tranquility, Simplicity, Joy

LAO TZU (C. 600 BC)

Lao Tzu, translated as "Old Master" or "Sage," was the Chinese Taoist philosopher who represents the very face and concept of reason, patience, and logic. His essence of such wisdom epitomizes the very spirit of tranquility in the context of the Theban Oracle. Although much of this ancient master remains a mystery, his lessons of wisdom and common sense continue to inspire those on the path to personal growth and understanding.

Recognized as the author of the *Tao Te Ching*, the classic philosophy in which "the manner of all life is to be used wisely by men and women" is the simple mind-set that is still very much in practice today. Believing that the human condition is similar to all things in the universe, and constantly being influenced by outside forces, makes it logical to believe that "simplicity" and living in an honest, calm, and modest manner will be the key to personal freedom, truth, and spiritual bliss.

Lao Tzu's philosophy was designed to remain as natural to men and women as possible, where all may live by the code of decency, respect, and honor. Believing that one's demeanor should be managed by his conscience, in fact knowing right from wrong, must be the simple path to pursue. He would always encourage his followers to observe everything in their surroundings, and then to endeavor the reasoning found in nature.

Legend dictates that the wise Lao Tzu became dismayed by the gross wickedness of men and retreated to the desert for solitude, leaving civilization behind. As he was leaving the gates of the kingdom, several of his followers persuaded the master to record the doctrine of his philosophies so they would not forget. The weary sage agreed and returned with the *Tao Te Ching* scroll, which contains eighty-one brief words of wisdom. This ancient Chinese text remains one of the world's most beloved tomes, revered by all those who desire to know peace and enlightenment in their lives, king and common man alike.

As time progressed, and the wise Lao Tzu lapsed into antiquity, the wisdom of the *Tao Te Ching* remained steadfast through the ages.

The simple words that echo an oasis of stillness and reflection, even when faced by upheaval and war, remain as true today as they did in ancient history. Yet this wisdom will only be discovered for those who truly seek its gentle messages.

DIVINATORY MEANINGS

In the context of this Theban Oracle, one might go by the mottos "Don't sweat the small stuff" and "Let go and let be," quite literally. Indeed, the teachings of Lao Tzu might very well be practiced on a daily basis as a simple way of life. With such quotes as "Stop thinking and end your problems," the soul of Lao Tzu's wisdom becomes clear. In short, this Theban stone declares that you are reaching full circle within a profound area of your inner condition, which may translate to: Relax and let the joy of simplicity take over. Now is the time to receive blessings that are appearing to you, without delay or guilt. Whether these blessings are material in nature, or simply divine understanding within your emotional structures, you are in line to receive a heightened sense of emotional contentment. Rejoice and be still in your sacred gain.

Because Lao Tzu remained true to a simple pattern in life, he was devoid of material and worldly desires beyond the essentials of unpretentious living. This simplicity was as natural to him as receiving air, food, and water for sustenance. Of course, the wisdom of Taoism is often placed in an atmosphere of the metaphysical, yet the old sage would simply have instructed that you relax, notice your surroundings, and be one with nature, as only then will you come to understand what you need to understand.

This Theban Oracle observes a new pattern emerging, where old habits will begin to wane. This stone instructs the bearer to heed the advice of the Taoist master and simply let the rays of joy and universal understanding, which is truly divine, to enter your sphere of being. For a moment, simply let go, if only to experience the pleasures of the meanings with a stress-free contentment.

The nature of this oracle gently suggests that you remove yourself from the everyday grind, to walk outside the blur of our technological and busy world. Take a walk outside and sit on the grass. Gaze at the simple movements of the clouds, and know that where they flow, they flow with both a mystical sense of purpose and an unknowing reason together; where such natural chaos is what is. Likewise, observe the stars that remain as steadfast as they have since the dawn of time, and know that even in the ever-expanding, ever-evolving universe, you too have such a divine yet simple purpose and reason, and that such things will happen in unison once you let go and let be.

A Stone Faced in Reverse

If you find the *Lao Tzu Theban Stone* faced away from you, then you may be in need of a change, though not necessarily a big change. Perhaps as the aforementioned advice offered, simply learn to relax. If your plans are not coming to fruition as hoped, you may wish to direct your efforts elsewhere for a while. It may be time to take a mental health day and sit this one out.

Because our world is becoming more and more stressful, and actually taking a holiday from such stresses is becoming more and more difficult, it may be time to take the wisdom of Lao Tzu and turn away from these stresses, even if only for a while. Although this does not mean that you must retreat to the desert as Lao Tzu did, you may need to drop off-screen for a while and simply relax, even if it means soaking in a hot bath, surrounded only by the lights of candles. Now might be a good time. Simply said, the universe may be suggesting you search for emptiness now, as only with this will you receive tranquility, which is needed above all. Meditation on the shores of a deserted beach, or sitting among the tall trees in a quiet forest, would do a world of good for you. You are formally requested to temporarily abandon the trappings of our modern civilization and return to the sense of our ancestors.

The computerized gadgets and technological idols must be put away, if only to be spared for a short time. It is time to receive what is rightfully yours, but you must first be willing to take this joy. Patience, meditation, and clarity about what lies around you are the medicines needed now. Accept that what fortunes come to you are richly deserved. Relax and enjoy.

The True Male Significance, Divine Silence, Emotional Transition

IMHOTEP (2667–2648 BC)

One of the most intriguing names in the realms of magick and sorcery is that of the ancient Egyptian magus known as *Imhotep*. His name meaning "the one who comes in peace," Imhotep was one of the first known architects to have erected the first pyramid. Though Hollywood and fiction writers describe this brilliant soul as an evil, supernatural monster, he is believed to have been a wise and kindly magus by most historical and archaeological scholars today.

In life, Imhotep was a physician, a scribe, and a chancellor to the pharaoh of Lower Egypt, as well as being a high priest of the Third Dynasty, during the reign of the kindly Pharaoh Netjerikhet. In addition to these elevated titles, he was also the court sage and poet, as well as astrologer and vizier under four separate pharaohs, which without a doubt relates a life of great honor and status. Because history offers little factual evidence to support either a malevolent nature or a persona of goodness, he has been added to the posture of *divine silence*, in the context of the Theban Oracle, which is synonymous with the enigma within the male significance.

Since the very image of Imhotep is one of mystery, we must accept the ancient papyrus and stone tablets that speak highly of him, understanding that such an enlightened personality must have been prudent to have survived the wrath of the many pharaohs he served. Because Imhotep is understood as being wise, enigmatic, and strangely veiled in the history of the ages, he is assigned the dubious placement of *true male significance* and *emotional transition* within the perspective of this divination system.

DIVINATORY MEANINGS

The *Imhotep Theban Stone* represents an almost enchanted sense of self-control and the elevated need for keeping the self and all its passions under control. Drawing this stone signifies that a time of emotional transition is in motion now. Although this unforeseen transition may be silent in its approach and concealed to loud, overly vocal, and emotionally immature people, a psychic shift is taking place for you now. This may produce uncanny emotions, yet with reverence for the mind-set of this ancient magus and scholar, such transitions may prove to be most enlightening.

This Theban stone may also relate that an inner storm may soon approach, a storm of your passions and often hidden emotions that must surface. Now is the time to be soulfully reflective while you are controlling these passions, which if not controlled properly may result in tensions between friend and family alike. Therefore, trust in yourself to be patient and sincere at all times and let this process complete itself naturally. Furthermore, if this flux of transition is too stressful, your physical body may be craving diversion or distraction. Taking a walk on a nature path, going for a brisk swim, or taking a trip to your local museum are all good examples of exercising both your body and intellect.

In truth, this is a time of great introspection and even joy. Although challenge and adjustment are customary for such emotional and soulful transitions, the outcome will be favorable, offering new opportunity and wisdom as the reward for being steadfast throughout this time in your life. Whether you are a man or a woman, it is time to reveal the spiritual warrior that lies within you and confront the trifling hobgoblins that hide in the recesses of your emotional mythology. Take that walk through your inner landscape that you hide, and see what you find there.

A STONE FACED IN REVERSE

When the *Imhotep Theban Stone* is drawn facing away from you, it signifies that your emotional state is in question. You may have too much of a load on the back of your spiritual and emotional self. Lighten the load a bit, and ease up on your daily stress as much as your life allows; and if your life does not allow for that, then do it anyway. Because this oracle refers to the delicate tissues of your inner self, the importance of relaxing and breathing properly becomes evident. The *Imhotep Theban Stone* advises that you think about your health, both physically and emotionally, as doing so will allow for positive growth and healthy contentment.

Observe the burdens you have been carrying lately, as well as the burdens of other people's issues you have elected to take on. Some may be taking advantage of you now, either deliberately or without knowing it. Because the weight of other people's stress may become too much for you, it may be only a matter of time until you stumble and fall. Even if this weight originates from friends or family, you must take a break now. If you fail to do so, the body may react negatively against you—making you sick, causing long-term ailments, and even worse—so the issue at hand should be clear for you. Step away, show self-restraint, and ease up a bit. Your true friends will understand and stay by your side through it all.

Darkness and Light, Coexisting Differences, Misconception, Judgment

HONORIUS OF THEBES
(C. 13TH CENTURY)

Signifying the highest example of the good bearing a shadow of evil, and the true evil shadowing the truth of good, this Theban stone exemplifies the historical enigma of *Honorius of Thebes*, the mysterious sage who defies historians worldwide. Assumed to be the creator of the Theban alphabet—designed to elude the murderous forces of the ancient Church—this mystical magus, the son of Euclid, remains the quintessential icon of Middle Age magick and the unknown. Remembered for being chosen by a council of occult masters from across Europe, Honorius of Thebes wrote seven volumes with ninety-three chapters on the magickal arts, known as *Liber Juratus*, or *The Sworne Booke of Honorius.* Over the centuries, however, only a few fragments of these sacred tomes remain intact, and with the enigma of this intriguing tome lingers the ether of strangeness, misconception, and misunderstanding.

Through the ages this historical figure bestowed a gift of the arcane, influencing a select few from various sacred orders far and wide to search for its meaning. From the scholarly wizard to the cunning witch, the fabled works of *The Sworne Booke of Honorius* had drifted from fact to fantasy, engaging those of goodly outlook and malevolent demeanor alike. Though the Master of the Thebans will no doubt remain as illusive in our future as he has been for these past centuries, we may take from his wisdom of the ages, for without such secret coding and ciphering, which was demanded of him, truly such honored collections would have been lost forever to the flames of inanity and detestation.

Because this historical figure illuminates both a shadow of darkness, giving the illusion of the sinister, as well as the light, promising hope and scholarly longevity, we must look upon his presence as the unattainable obscurity within a shroud of mystery. And, as this Theban stone represents both the light and the darkness, or that which contains both the elements of good and evil, it is thus rendered the honor of a unique presence in the context of the Theban Oracle and its perspective.

DIVINATORY MEANINGS

This Theban stone embraces the concept of both light and darkness, where both reveal very different realities when viewed separately. As a sculpture that is crafted to show the beauty of its features may resonate elegance during the garish light of day, or may take on a sinister quality by night, our perspectives create two distinct worlds to choose from. Though in truth that sculpture takes on no new features, it does nevertheless appears to change with the absence of light. This oracle relates the ideal that there are many aspects of what we call truth, which may differ greatly depending on one's point of view. For what may appear as virtuous and kind to some may seem shameless and evil to others. It's all a matter of perspective and personal choice.

As with all things under the heavens, there are battles taking place. There may be a spiritual battle taking place within you now. There may even be those who see you as something other than who you truly are. Be still now. Though the truth may be hidden from those who wish not to peer long and hard on your character, another will see you for who you truly are, and from there a flower may blossom full and true. Endurance and faith are all you need. This Theban stone offers you this simple reality: "Let heaven do its work now, be patient throughout its process, and trust that all will be well in the end."

Like the historically mysterious Honorius of Thebes—whose enigmatic reputation had him appearing saintly and helpful to some but evil and blasphemous to others—here too is where you stand with a present situation. Although you may indeed be doing the most good, another may see your efforts as being the opposite. It is time to be mindful and willing to continue on your spiritual passage, being devoid of anxiety and mistrust. You are ready and aware now.

Prepare to do what is appropriate, regardless of the way others see or judge you. Your spiritual gallantry and moral dedication will not go unnoticed, for your philosophical courage tells you that there is no try, only do. Your task now is to be mentally, emotionally, and spiritually prepared to complete your endeavors without doubt. You are filled with the light of commitment, which enables you to carry on regardless of any darkness that may cast doubtful shadows on you and your works. You know the truth, and you know what you must do. Your journey has begun.

A STONE FACED IN REVERSE

When this Theban Stone is drawn faced away from you, it asks you to examine all of your motives with clear thought and meaningful intent. It is asking you to contemplate your affairs now, as you may be putting too much effort into any one situation or goal. You may be trying too hard to convince someone who is misjudging you, giving all your efforts to a fruitless cause. Perhaps you're putting too much effort into a person or group of people in order to change their opinions about you. Perhaps you have been placed in a dark position because of another's ignorance or lack of self-worth. And, though this may feel degrading and hurtful, remember that this too is an acceptable instance in the grand scheme of things. But adjusting for another's conception of who you truly are will only delay such truth and eventually waste your energy.

The *Honorius of Thebes Stone* in reverse warns of the dangers of poor synchronicity, and not adhering to what is needed for you and you alone. Maintaining good judgment regarding the time you give, how much of that time, and when you offer it is in question now. You may be expending far too much energy on a subject or person. Be caring and show respect, but do not allow yourself to become a spiritual doormat, for those who would paint a false portrait of you will gladly take what you offer, leaving you empty and spiritually shaken. In the end, either you will be content with yourself, regardless of the spiritual shade you bear, or you will waste away from the spiritual and emotional parasites of those who would misjudge you in spite of the good that you do. Choose, but choose wisely.

Cherubic Protection, Security, Divine Mortality

ALBERTUS MAGNUS (C. 1206–1280)

This famed 13th-century Dominican friar and tutor in the sciences of alchemy, chemistry, and metaphysics serves as the fundamental symbol for divine protection and security in the context of the Theban Oracle. *Albertus Magnus*, although to become the Bishop of Regensburg and later canonized as Saint Albert the Great, was nonetheless one of the most noble magi in history. Most noted for being an advocate for a peaceful coexistence between science, religion, and magick, this skilled scholar had made considerable progress in a time of strife and religious slavery. He had secured for himself a place of distinction and honor, holding great regard even to this day.

Believed by some to have coined the concept of a "New Age," Albertus Magnus believed mankind would one day rise out of the ashes of despair to become a more noble and peaceful creature. In his *Book of Secrets*, Magnus referred to this New Age as a place in time when all people could live together in harmony regardless of any particular ideological, religious, or philosophical differences. Although this unconventional notion would not come into a philosophical light until much later in history, his ideals were astonishing nonetheless. He had a firm belief that all things in nature—whether humans, animals, plants, the oceans, crystalline minerals, or even the air—somehow aid in one's emotional and psychic powers. Undeniably, these principles had a profound effect on his society, both for the layman and practitioner of high magick, attracting scholars from far and wide to his unique teachings.

Instructing from the ancient intellectuals before him, such as Aristotle, Plato, and Galen, Albertus Magnus applied their wise perspectives to his own academic milieu. He then taught that the lives of all living things were naturally manipulated by the grand interrelationships of the stars and planets, whereby each and every aspect of the human condition was prompted by the divine movements of the universe. Indeed, his most famous student, Thomas Aquinas, would follow his lead and carry on these advanced philosophical traditions for the rest of his life.

This scholarly and gentle magus made it possible for those thirsting for wisdom to drink from the fountain of clear thought—which overflowed with simplicity—and being devoid of oppression and stagnation, only those with an inner determination would gain and transform from these time-honored lessons. This Theban stone represents the sacred act of producing a sense of compassion and love, which are formally interwoven within the arena of high spiritualism.

DIVINATORY MEANINGS

This is the Theban stone that best symbolizes release and renewed understanding. This oracle foretells that an intellectual or philosophical fog will be lifting soon from your life. It tells you that a time-honored tradition may be coming to a close, that there will soon be a release from a negative or painful function to a new and positive role. Because the main element of this oracle relates "Cherubic" protection, literally translated as the workings of angels, you can rest assured that this oracle is true, and that there will indeed be a releasing from an old pattern to the new. Much like Albertus Magnus, who applied the right amount of resolve in leading others out of the darkness of their thinking habits, here too will you find refuge within a new philosophy. This is truly a time to rejoice.

When there is understanding and acceptance of any situation we face in life, a feeling of security floods the foundations of our psychic constitution. And, as a byproduct to this divine leap of faith, you are afforded a lifelong education in the process. Be aware, however, that concentration and a serious outlook are in order here. Remember, if you go blindly into any situation or life event without spiritual substance, you are bound to stumble and fall. In short, take the time to mentally and spiritually visualize the path before you, before you begin your journey. Mindfully avoid the old obstacles and stumbling blocks that once stood in your way, and proceed. You will see clearly now, once you let your "psychic vision" adjust to the darkness and the outdated trappings of your former spiritual landscapes. Once done, you will see those stumbling blocks and pitfalls and progress. A new wisdom is assured.

A Stone Faced in Reverse

When the *Albertus Magnus Theban Stone* is drawn faced away, do not panic. It does not imply that you will be plunging into a thick fog of confusion or a pit of spiritual darkness. This stone is merely telling you to slow down and take a second look at your situation. It's simply telling you that nothing is easy, and not to become discouraged in whatever arises. Think about how difficult it must have been for 13th-century people to comprehend and trust in the concepts of a metaphysical or New Age world when the common beliefs were so tainted with ignorance. Yet a select few were able to gaze beyond the confines of such small thinking and take that leap of faith, which culminated in divine understanding and spiritual enlightenment.

You may see this oracle's example in any number of realities. Perhaps it is referring to stagnation within a friendship or romantic relationship, perhaps suggesting that a way of life that has been trusted for so many years is simply not yielding the same feelings of contentment. Although sounding dire, the meaning is simply to release the old tradition that is holding you in place or making you stumble. Now is the time for spiritual progression. You have divine permission to move on.

Now is the time to ask yourself: Are you holding on to this stagnation or spiritual weight for a good reason, and is your sacrifice done for anything other than truly noble gains? These are the inward questions being asked of you now, so keep in mind that without total honesty and compliance with the issues at hand, you simply cannot proceed. Take the needed time to step away from this situation or problem and think. Emotionally, spiritually, and with heart, beseech the heavens for the right choices now, as not doing so will only delay you from where you need to be.

ɱ
ɧ

A Portal or Entrance, an Elevated Transposition

MERLIN (C. 6TH CENTURY)

Very few are unaware of the *Merlin* legend, the scholarly hermit-like magus who tutored and aided a young boy named Arthur to become king of the ancient isles of Britannia. Almost everyone can recall the image of the wise sage who dressed in rags, walked with a staff, and talked to all of nature. Perceived as the kindly and mysterious teacher with great mystical powers, this age-old image continues to inspire and direct the wizard-to-be, even today.

While the majority of what we have heard about this historical wizard is largely incorrect by way of Hollywood and similar storytellers, what many scholars do suspect as truth is a mixture of the many legends we have heard over the centuries. From the Druidic priest and prophetic wild man of the archaic Roman-ruled isles, to the wise and chivalric sage Myrddin as depicted by the scholar Sir Geoffrey of Monmouth, the man who came to be known as Merlinus—the legend in all his guises had secured for himself a place in history. Indeed, this internationally celebrated wizard plays a crucial role in the quintessential representation of goodly magick and wisdom, as well as being an icon for modern practitioners of the old religion.

During the Middle Ages the Merlin legend became very popular, becoming the central figure in the 13th-century Anglo-Saxon and French literary cycles. The English author and researcher Sir Thomas Malory further immortalized the Merlin persona centuries later with his *Le Morte d'Arthur*, presenting him as the moral and cerebral advisor to the future king. In Lord Tennyson's *The Idylls of the King*, we see the Merlin character as the grand architect of Camelot and all-around patriarch whom all respected and honored. Undeniably, as time proceeded and cultures modernized, so did the legend of this enigmatic wizard.

In whatever arena one places the wise magus Merlin—be it as Arthur's advisor and prophet, or as the romantically colored 12th-century magician who instructed Uther Pendragon in the rules of battle and the values of governing, or who oversaw the positioning of the massive megalithic boulders of Stonehenge—most accept that this man did indeed live. Whether or not he was an actual figure as accounted for by the 9th-century chronicler *Nennius*—who tells of such a man who was born without a human father, and who had prophesied the defeat of Britannia by the hoarding Saxons—is of no concern among the enlightened. He is as real as the sun and the moon, where his wisdom and teachings continue to serve the willing regardless of his historical wiles.

DIVINATORY MEANINGS

Like the elusive wizard who walked from one reality to another, proving to be the archetypal image of wisdom for every age of the truth seeker and those searching for enlightenment, the *Merlin Theban Stone* represents the natural laws of change, which are always in transition. From birth, life, death, and decay, to rebirth and life renewed, this stone stands for a mystifying portal that serves as both an exit and as an entrance, where the realities of both life and death coexist in harmony.

The *Merlin Theban Stone* expresses that once you have gone through a door, you are now ready to transverse through another. This stone relates that there will be both a death and a birth soon to arise—an ending and a beginning. Though this does not signify an actual physical death or birth, drawing this stone indicates that the everyday lifestyle you have been living has come to, or is about to come to, a close, even if you are unaware of such a transition.

This oracle advises that resisting the inevitable will only delay what naturally needs to take place. Whether this refers to a relationship or life situation, it is time to weigh all the values that have been accumulated during your past journeys. Take this time to identify the positive change and growth that has taken place over the years, doing the same with the level of stagnation and loss. How does it all add up? Although letting go of the old and outdated things will surely involve a seemingly dark and foreboding voyage into the rough spiritual waters of the unknown, know that your very life, regardless of the crashing waves of doubt and fear that may follow, will eventually lead to a brighter and fresher place of spiritual being where perpetual renewal is always the outcome.

In both the physical and spiritual aspects of death, a vital and unseen energy is being released, which in turn mutates and travels to a new destination. It promotes new life by way of a birth, which then continues to offer the same over and over again. Whether in the physical sense or that of the spirit, this oracle relates the simple edict that one must depart one space before entering another. With this relatively undemanding transformational request, you should prepare yourself to take a much larger step in an even larger universe.

A Stone Faced in Reverse

Drawing the *Merlin Theban Stone* faced away indicates a hesitation to abide by the natural laws of release. It signifies that you may know that change is inevitable yet choose not to listen to your intuition.

Choosing not to hear the gentle calling for transformation, which is within you now, will only delay what is needed to take place in your life. This stone relates to a fear of the unknown. Though you may fear an issue or group of issues that are reasonably simple to comprehend and relinquish, you'll succeed if the proper actions are taken. You may need to consider this as an awakening, or as a claxon bell to be spiritually heard. Take this time to consider all that you have been denying. Listen to yourself with more insistence of heart than through logic alone.

Now is the time to turn away from the irrational fears that may be holding you in place, where you should be moving on. Like a darkened forest before you, the unrecognizable sounds echoing from within will naturally send a chill through you. Even if you know there is nothing to fear; you still fear. Instead of shying away, simply enter that dark and seemingly scary forest, where in truth, the imaginary monsters that dwell there fear you far more than you might expect. Let go now and walk forward, knowing in your heart that you will reach the other side without incident or failure. Instead of the frightening creatures you think may be lurking within, simply know that the only things surrounding you are the fragrant pines and the gentle spirit of the great Merlin himself.

Know that this Theban Oracle simply suggests that now is the time to walk through the life-altering doorway that stands before you. It is telling you not to fear, as what lies beyond this portal is far less alarming than you might think.

Ending Stone

Ending to a Life Process, Life Transition, Concurrence

DIVINATORY MEANINGS

This Theban stone represents and signifies the ending to a life cycle, or process, as well as a transition or a concurrence within one's personal circumstances. This may signify that you're finished with something in your life, referring to a precise question or to the recent outcome of an earlier situation. The *Theban Ending Stone* or "period stone," as it is viewed in the context of the Theban Oracle, exemplifies that some aspect to your life is indeed coming to a close, or transitioning to another place, whether spiritually, emotionally, or physically. It may represent forming a union with another aspect of your existence. As such can represent a very deep and complicated situation, you are advised to look deeply within yourself and contemplate before moving.

This Theban stone represents that which cannot see, read, hear or instruct, yet it represents all of these things at the same time regardless. Although a conundrum, its purpose signifies the cryptic realities of life, death, and rebirth. When drawing this Theban stone, you are required to sit a moment and reflect on the stones you have already drawn during the oracle process. Realize the significance in a manner that only you can, by being still and reflective. Moreover, you should not draw another stone right away, especially if you do not "feel" you should. By this I mean: Consider not forcing an answer, as doing so will only foster a hurried response, which may not be correct. Be patient.

A Stone Faced in Reverse

When drawing this Theban stone faced away, or if drawn as part of a question that is abundant with many unambiguous patterns, look again at the stones you have already drawn, and think about them. If you wish, you may forfeit this Theban stone by placing it back into an accompanying bag, gently agitating and then redrawing for the possible answer to your question. If, however, this Theban stone was drawn as a *daily one stone draw*, then this oracle is indeed giving you its response. Simply walk away and ask no more questions for that day. In short, it's plain to see the almost daunting demeanor this Theban stone embellishes. Although one might see the worst in its initial cryptic representations, simply take it as a chance to rethink something, rather than being a dreadful warning.

This stone represents something special. Consider the amazing with this stone!

Mystery Stone

An Unknowable Path, the Mystery of Arcane Origins, Spiritual Freedom

BETHANY (CA. 1800)

When this Theban stone is drawn, either faced up, faced down, or turned away, it signifies the great mystery of your life. This stone is dedicated to *Bethany*, an enigmatically elusive New England woman of the early 1800s. Though almost nothing is known of this interesting historical figure, she symbolizes the mystery of an unknowable origin, as well as the path she had taken in her earthly incarnation. Today, her past shares with us the value of secrecy she had to endure during her day. And though she lived in an age of professed enlightenment, religious freedoms were not entirely ensured, forcing her to progress in silence and anonymity.

Believed to have lived in a small township in a remote section of Maine, evidence suggests that she had practiced as a goodly spell crafter and magickal herbalist. Moreover, with the discovery of her *Book of Shadows*—which shows her particular genius and creativeness for the craft, as well as her singular understanding of the arcane aspects of magick—her placement among the honored, regardless of her ambiguity, is assured in the context of the Theban Oracle.

The historically inscrutable woman known as Bethany should be remembered for her contributions to both her secret and public lifestyles, which must have been agonizingly rife with fear and guilt. Where publicly she most assuredly represented the quintessential Victorian-age woman, full of proud virtues and silent suffering, she nonetheless managed to delve in the magickal arts in spite of the totalitarian attitudes and suffocating belief systems of her day. Indeed, she should serve as an icon of women's rights, religious freedoms, and free thinking for the modern-day practitioner of all faiths.

As Bethany's apparent wisdom had also entered the realms of high magick, using ancient astrological formats and rituals of the Kabbalah, she also probed into many secret writing systems, such as celestial glyphs, herbal associations and iconology, and most notably the Theban script. Within her decaying *Book of Shadows*, the tattered and mold-stained remains showed various aspects of the Theban alphabet as applied to the rituals she had once taken part in. Although Bethany's true place in her society, her nature and personality, and even her very image remain a mystery, we must realize the great strides she took, her silent contribution to the practice of free thought, and the positive examples she left with us today. For these noble reasons, this Theban stone is so dedicated to Bethany.

DIVINATORY MEANINGS

The *Bethany Theban Stone* represents the arcane mystery, which coexists alongside reason and understanding. It exemplifies the mystery of the unknowable path that all of us assume throughout our daily lives. Though we may operate through a definite structure and principle throughout our waking lives, following a path that is understood and accepted in our everyday existence, we may nonetheless be dumbfounded by the understanding of our spiritual selves.

Understanding these realities, which are in truth a vast and difficult universe to chart within us, is one of the first vital steps to spiritual freedom, should we encounter the amazing. Once you understand that there is a gentle but persistent wind blowing throughout your spiritual self, thus releasing the sacred aspects of your essence to travel down an unseen path that lies ahead, this is your first vital step toward spiritual awakening. Letting go of the unnecessary baggage, the emotional and spiritual garbage that clutters this path, is the second vital step. The third and final step is for you to step back and firmly give thanks to that vast internal universe that has always coexisted within you. Knowing that such greatness exists throughout the mysterious self, which eludes us during our conscious state, is in fact our greatest ally.

The primary reasoning behind this stone simply points to the most important realities within the complex nature of the human condition. The realities of self-acceptance, self-realization, and self-love are the basic elements that require the most nourishment. Before we release the garbage and baggage that cling to us, we must first identify them for what they are. Only then can spiritual freedom be obtained.

This Theban stone equates the whole of the self, which is almost never realized by those who do not believe in themselves or their heavenly purpose in life. In short, it signifies the initiation of your soul to a higher level of reality. The enigmatic Bethany, who lived in a questionable time rife with small thinking and ignorance, nonetheless rose above what others would have allowed her. For even more than the mysteries she had discovered of the unknown, she discovered far more about herself in the process. Now is the time to heed her example by *trusting, believing,* and most of all, *loving* yourself entirely. Unless you're fully committed to those three simple requests, your journey will always be littered with that unwanted emotional and spiritual rubbish that is keeping you from understanding yourself fully. It's time to clean your spiritual temple and partake of that unknowable journey that lies ahead.

Chapter Five

MEDIEVAL METAPHYSICS AND THE QUEST FOR TRUTH AND ENLIGHTENMENT

Now that your introduction to Medieval metaphysics and the Theban Oracle is coming to a close—having learned some of the basics about the mysterious realities of ancient ceremonial magick, divination systems, and the notable luminaries who created them—you are now ready to take your first steps within a vast and somewhat hidden universe. Although the possibilities of where this process can lead a student of Medieval metaphysics are virtually limitless, the inner journey that has begun must be one of studious exploration and true belief in order to culminate in victory. Indeed, if one brings true sincerity into such possibilities, the end product can be as noble and as spiritually enlightening as any wizard or sage could ever desire.

The Theban stones and the heartfelt meanings that coexist within them are, in truth, of you and you alone. The magick you seek has been within you all along. There is no mystery. Though the historically enigmatic Honorius of Thebes may have given the world a true mystery as to the correct and purposeful implications found within *The Sworne Booke of Honorius,* the innermost meaning should at least be somewhat clear for us. And even though the ramifications of the exquisite Theban alphabet continue to misguide and confuse scholar and novice alike, the simple equation nonetheless continues to be found by the beholder. Whether we will ever have the chance to view the many ancient tomes and fragments of antediluvian scrolls is of no concern, for if these ancient words of mysticism were nothing more than many falsehoods, the truth of one's self will continue to endeavor regardless, so long as the human spirit continues to yearn for answers to the many mysteries that continue to confound us.

When using the Theban stones, understand that this book serves as a beginning for something truly enlightening. Although in the grand scheme of all things magickal, the lessons found here are the tip of the iceberg, with each step that you explore the avenues and alleyways of our truly magickal universe, the more you'll become aware of the infinite realities that often go unnoticed. Now, you must trust yourself to continuously add to this wellspring of wisdom, in effect adding your own personality, demeanor, and spiritual circumference when partaking in the hidden wisdom that you will no doubt discover.

Because the study of such arcane wisdom requires steady and tenacious effort within the realms of our collegiate temples and beyond, mastering such concepts will require an equal amount of both faith and willpower in order to succeed. To truly comprehend the meanings of the ancients, you will have to step back and lower any purposeful intellect, as well as the typical education you may have gleaned over the years, and be still. Simply said, we must forfeit our human prides and prejudices and become the student once again in order to hear the distant lessons from the masters of old.

In the arenas of magick and the metaphysical—whether it is within the more elementally pagan faiths, or that akin to the scientific aspects of magick such as alchemy and astrology, or perhaps from a more religious point of view, like that of traditional ceremonial magick—you'll find a place for this oracle and its presentation of higher consciousness and related doctrines and disciplines. Because we as a people must remember our roots, so as not to repeat the same mistakes over and over again, we must actively search, recognize, isolate, and truly engage in understanding what mysteries stand before us, before we make any undue judgment or condemnation. This is the vital edict for all who partake in this and similar journeys that travel upon the sacred pathways.

The Theban stone oracle, although a relatively new concept in relation to the many known oraclelike processes, is really quite simple in relation to flow and comprehension of simple wisdom. It is designed to bring about a goodly feeling to that of the misunderstood beliefs regarding magick and comparative religions. Indeed, with the hate-filled delusions of the uneducated who see those who yearn for such knowledge as loathsome or evil, they themselves will fall prone to their own accusations. Remember, the dark avatars and devils seen by those who simply choose not to learn or understand are assembled from the collected memories of half-formed bedtime stories and childish warnings. We will know better.

As you progress with *The Theban Oracle*, you'll begin to understand and actually feel the natural rhythm and vibrations through the stones. More important, you'll begin to realize that you have a kind of wisdom, not unlike that of the magi and sages of ancient history. Trust in the process that appears to you. Take your time, never pushing or hurrying this process, and above all, always believe in yourself.

Chapter Six

USING the THEBAN STONES
for GOODLY
SPELL CASTING

Seeing there is a threefold world, elementary, celestial and intellectual, and every

inferior is governed by its superior, and receiveth the influence of the virtues

thereof, so that the very original and chief worker of all doth by angels, the

heavens, stars, elements, animals, plants, metals and stones convey from himself

the virtues of his omnipotency upon us . . .

CORNELIUS AGRIPPA, *THREE BOOKS OF OCCULT PHILOSOPHY*, BK. I, CHAP. I

From this simple yet eloquent passage, Cornelius Agrippa offers us a perspective on all areas of magick and spell crafting. Surely, Agrippa saw within all things a living, sentient intelligence, and respected the simple laws of nature when engaging in the magickal arts. Here too must we abide by such laws and hold an ample amount of said respect in order to successfully manifest our goodly desires.

This section of the Theban experience relates to all things spiritual and magickal, where you the diviner and spell caster will have sufficient wisdom to either begin or continue your quest into the realities of the wizard, the witch, or the sage. With that said, take these Theban examples of simple spell craft and apply them to your ritual or meditative practice with the secure knowledge that such things will be respectable and forthcoming. Truly believe in your innate powers; whether sagacious or apprentice, you will create positive change for yourself, as only *true* belief will be the very quintessence you will need within the realms of magick.

Because Agrippa and his contemporaries believed that the magickal essentials of our world were composed of five basic elements—Fire, Air, Water, Earth, and Spirit within the earthly and celestial realms, and also consisting of angels and cosmic intelligences—we can direct our magickal efforts in much the same manners as the many luminaries depicted in this book. In this context, I have applied the use of the Theban script to empower and identify the magickal spells that will proceed. By simply applying the time-honored and rudimentary fundamentals to these simple spells that are uniquely united with a true belief that your magick will work, you will indeed be successful.

Below, you will find several basic works of Theban magick, which will be as easy to accomplish as you see fit. The spell crafting and candle magick listed here regards simple yet eloquent examples of enchantment for issues of the heart, for protection and guidance, for banishing negativity, and for letting go of unwanted hardships that attach themselves to body, mind, and soul, as well as to the home. All, however, are designed to aid the development of wisdom, which is within yourself. Therefore, embrace the good and honest rewards you desire, and know that these are meant for you and the ones you love.

Spells and Rituals for Love-Related Issues

The desire for love is the quintessential aspect of the human condition. Indeed, this thing we call love—which may be seen as the way a mother loves her child, or as the child loves his or her beloved pet, or the romantic admirations we experience—is in every fiber of our existence. It is understandable for the unseen reality of love and compassion to weigh heavy on the spirit. We see the elements of this most natural desire to mingle deeply in the many aspects of our waking lives. Be it in the many ballads we hear each day on the radio, or as the primary ingredients for books and films, we are surrounded by the enigmatic force we call love.

When delving into the realms of magick for securing love and companionship, it is vital to remember a few simple laws. The first law is never to force one's will and desire upon another. By this I mean selecting any given person to fall in love with you by magickal means. By doing so, you tamper with the unforeseen passions of another by bending their will, and with their need to have love themselves. Although doing so requires great skill and willpower in itself, it is not wholly impossible to do. The problem in doing so is that it will be full of strife and complication, and will not last. If love is truly not meant to be, it simply will not be so. You and I may be able to force our hand in love by such methods, but it will be fruitless and cheerless.

The second law is to never focus on any one person. By this, I refer to any sympathetic guided-focusing techniques, otherwise known as "treasure mapping." In some instances, like personal goals and desires, many will place photographic or illustrated objects on a poster board surrounded by religious icons such as a crucifix or perhaps an image like the Buddha in order in enhance the will of the divine to make your wishes come true. Although such methods may very well work, when it is applied to someone who is not already in love with you, you may tempt their unwanted passions and create a negative outcome in the process.

The final law may be the most difficult for many to adhere to. This law pertains to one's objective and to their ideals of love. Is it love or lust for which you search? Is this love for personal gain, or is it for true, romantic, and sharing companionship? These questions are the most important because what you truly desire may make the difference between true happiness and misery.

The following spell craft is intended to be applied to the most true and honest of goals and outcomes. It is designed for the inner magick that all of us have within us, which is always ready for either our benefit or destruction. Understanding and respecting the afore-mentioned laws will only aid you in your goodly works of spell craft. Only true belief in oneself will blossom forth the results you truly deserve.

THEBAN SPELL FOR FINDING TRUE LOVE

This first spell is reasonably simple, as it requires only a few materials. First, you will need some articles representative of love. These things can represent many separate and distinct items, but for this spell, I have added only the most potent.

For this spell, you will need:

1. Several white roses or any other flowers that are most closely aligned to romance and affection for you, the spell crafter. Flowers such as jasmine, gardenia and orris root works well.

2. An article from your body, such as a few strands of hair, fingernail clippings, or a scrap of your old clothing.

3. A small piece of parchment paper and red ink, specifically Dove's Blood Ink, a quill or writing stylus. Both can be purchased at most New Age stores.

4. Dragon's Blood incense, in either powder or resin form, which may also be purchased at most New Age stores.

5. A foot or so of deep-red ribbon, cut to an angle at both ends.

6. A metal, ceramic, or glass bowl.

7. Ignitable charcoal for burning powder or resin incense.

8. An incense censer for burning powder or resin incense.

First, take the roses or other flowers and tie them with a small piece of the red ribbon; then hang these, tied upside down so that they will dry naturally. Do this on a Sunday evening at 5 o'clock and remove at 6 o'clock the following Sunday evening.

Take your flowers, still tied in the ribbon, and lay them on your altar. If you do not have an assigned altar, simply lay the flowers on a windowsill or table that faces north. In a small bowl, place a handful of the flower petals.

On the parchment paper, write a brief statement of what you're looking for in a true love, remembering that you must ask only for the most honorable of attributes. After this is done, you will kiss the parchment with good intent, then roll it up tightly, wrapping it with more of the red ribbon around the scroll, tying it in a knot. This will never again be opened. Now place this love scroll in front of the flower petals.

Once done, take the incense charcoal and light it. Once the charcoal is lit and glowing, place a small amount of the Dragon's Blood incense on top of it and let it smolder. As the smoke rises and the room is filled with the exotic and delightful scent, envision the man or woman of your dreams as completely as you can. Do this until the incense has burned away. Now take a little more of the incense and place it on the charcoal. This time, envision the qualities you desire in your dream love as completely as you can. Once done, give thanks to the heavens and say, "Now it is done; let what may be—be."

You may revisit this magickal method as often as you wish, but I give ample warning: Such spell craft must never be done with ill intent, or if you're simply not ready for love in your life. This spell has a powerful reputation for working quite efficiently, so be prepared for seeing the fruition of your desires here. Also, I must remind you that under no circumstance should you direct any "specifically known" person to this spell. By doing so, you may inevitably draw someone to you that should not be with you. And by doing so, you will be employing negative magick, and as the consequences are usually not pleasant, it is best to ask the wisdom of the heavens instead of that of lust, greed, or malice.

THEBAN SPELL TO RESTORE LOST LOVE

This spell for the restoration of lost love is identical to the one above, except here you will use the items that are directly related to the one you have lost. When the "magick" has gone out of a relationship, or if you wish to recapture the feelings that you once had, this spell will aid you in such pursuits. Although once again I advise against using force in such matters, what I do suggest is that you ask the counsel of the heavens. For when you humbly beseech for that which is best for you and the one you love, only the best and most worthy outcome will occur.

For this spell, you will need:

I. Two photographs of the two of you, preferably taken during happier times (e.g., wedding, vacation, or holiday photos).

2. A 9 x 9 inch square of pink or red cloth.

3. Several articles from both you and your love, such as fingernails, hair, or scraps of old clothing.

4. A foot or two of deep-red ribbon, cut to an angle at both ends.

5. One sheet of parchment paper.

6. Dove's Blood Ink and quill or writing stylus.

7. Dragon's Blood incense, in either powder or resin form.

8. One dried red or white rose.

9. Ignitable charcoal for burning powder or resin incense.

10. An incense censer for burning powder or resin incense.

First, take one of your photos and prop it up so you can look upon it while you work the ritual. Take the pink or red cloth and lay it in front of you; then sprinkle the dried petals from the rose across the cloth. Now add the articles from your body and from your love's, and set aside.

With quill and ink, write the reasons (as many as you want) why you want your love to come back to you; why you are worthy of his or her love, and what you are willing to sacrifice in order to have this love returned. At this point, light the Dragon's Blood incense and let it smolder, while at the same time, looking at the photo that you set up before you. Do this for a few moments, meditating on all the good things you remember about your lost love. Though sex may be one remembrance, try to visualize the more spiritual aspects of that relationship.

After a time, with the room filled with exotic smoke, take the parchment paper and fold it up as small as you can and then lay it on top of the cloth and rose petals. Now, lay the other photograph on top of that. Once done, take your ribbon, and with the quill and ink write your name at one end and the name of your true love at the other. Don't worry if you can't see it due to the corresponding colors; simply write the name and let it dry. When this is complete, fold the cloth and everything within it into a nice, neat bundle. Wrap the ribbon around the bundle, tying the ribbon at one end in three knots, repeating the words *Love, Honor,* and *Respect* with each knot.

When this is done, relight a little more of the Dragon's Blood incense and let it burn until gone. Take this bundle and place under your bed, leaving it there for three days and nights. If you have pets that like to chew on things, then you can tack it above your bedroom door instead of placing it beneath your bed. After the three days, place the bundle on your nightstand or dresser, place a framed photo of the two of you near the bundle, and surround it with more flowers. You may wish to burn a red or pink candle from time to time in order to draw forth the element of love and romance. Remember, if this lost love is not intended to be fruitful and re-emerge, then you must simply move on. You may certainly revisit this particular spell if you desire, but only your heart will know what is best to do.

Theban Incense and Oil Spells for Purification and Protection

As there are literally thousands of methods for blessing, protecting, and empowering one's self and home by means of magick, it would be almost impossible to list all of them. However, as nature holds within it all the powers needed to defeat and silence negativity and evil, I will include a few here.

Among the most common rituals used in ancient times was the power of divine smoke. In ancient Christendom the sacred smoke of the ignited resins of frankincense and myrrh were commonly burned to ward off evil spirits, and ground the church, temple, or sacred site as a holy place. In the temples of the Far East, from Tibet and India to the mosques of the Arabic nations, similar resins and incenses were burned for the same divine purposes. In Asian countries it is prominent to use smoke in many rituals of protection and clearing, as well as for assisting prayers and wishes in reaching the heavens and the departed. Indeed, in the Americas, these practices are also used. Whether it be for the clearing of negativity or for grounding a sacred space, the use of smoke is a common and respected ritual to this day.

The following incense rituals may be used at any time. For the employment of magick or for everyday practice, the reality of divine smoke will invigorate the senses and enthrall the spirit. The Theban associations herein may be applied in several formats. The first manner in which to use the Theban script is for a "placemat effect." Here, using either parchment paper or virgin cloth, the Theban symbols for the purposes of banishing negativity or instilling positive reinforcements into any place or object are made by simply writing the words of power. Words of power are any word or phrase that is designed to banish evil influences and negativity. Words like *Peace, Love,* and *Happiness Dwells Here* are all example of powerful words. Phrases like *Evil Be Gone* and *Let Only Truth and Love Live Here* are also good examples of powerful words and statements. To this end, you may also wish to employ the names of angels who serve various heavenly duties to these Theban placemats, as doing so will call upon their heavenly assistance. Either way, these placemats, when added to ritualistic incense burning, will add a stronger sense of purpose and reason to your magickal endeavors.

The Theban placemat ritual, although somewhat enigmatic for some magick workers, has ancient ties to magick, having its basis in sympathetic ritual. Because this incense "cleansing" format will serve countless situations, you may apply this ritual for any number of problems. The subsequent format may be used with a number of different resins and powdered herbs.

The incense rituals that follow are an example of the items you will need and how you should go about producing them. They will also offer ideas for how to carry out your own, individually designed rituals for any number of issues.

THEBAN NEGATIVITY CLEANSING INCENSE RITUAL

For this spell, you will need:

1. A brass, copper, silver, or steel bowl.

2. Several nuggets of myrrh resin, which can be purchased at most New Age stores.

3. Ignitable charcoal bricks.

4. A sheet of parchment paper or a sheet of natural undyed cotton.

5. Black Magic Marker.

6. Two candles, one black, one white. Small taper candles or votives will do nicely.

The sacred herbal resin of myrrh (*Comniphora myrrha*), which is derived from a native gum tree of the Far East, produces a rich and mysterious fragrance and is reputed to aid in the divine. When burned along with other resins, such as frankincense or copal, the combination manifests a strong feeling of grounding, as well as creating a state of celestial enlightenment. Burn this and a combination of the aforementioned resins for purification and protection rituals. This resin mixture will open the senses to the ethereal realms wherever you are.

To make the placemat, simply take a piece of parchment paper or virgin cloth, which is any piece of natural cloth such as undyed cotton or wool, cut into a square, and written upon it the Theban letter that corresponds to various actions and powers. For instance, the Theban letter *C*, represented by Zoroaster, is characterized by the powers of inner strength and divine understanding. If your ritual is to remove the negativity that has been plaguing your life or if you would want extra fortification in these areas, then you would write this letter at one point on your paper or cloth. Apply the problem that needs tending to the most at the highest point to your left, and continue to the right, then lower left, and lower right to assign four issues to the cleansing and positive fortification ritual. If, however, you are focusing on only one issue, simply write the Theban letter that best corresponds to your problem at the dead center of the paper or cloth. Now you're ready to begin.

With your placemat ready, face the top of the placemat toward the east. Set it upon your altar or on a table. Place your candles in the following order, white to the left side of your placemat, which will draw forth the negative energies, pushing them toward the center of the altar. Place the black candle to the right of the placemat, which will halt the negative energies, pushing them back to the center of the placemat. Once this is done, light the candles, starting from the left, then the right, always lighting the white first and black last.

As the candles are lit, let them burn for a few moments as you mentally focus on your issues and problems. Think about what you want done and how your life should be. Envision the outcome of your future before you. Believe it to be favorable and calm, beneficial and rewarding. You are successful and you are a winner, for there is nothing that can overtake your goodly desires and working. You are in control, and the heavens are supporting you. After a time, with the light of the candles burning bright, you're ready for the next step.

Light the ignitable charcoal brick until it turns bright red. Set the Myrrh nuggets to smolder on the charcoal brick and let the room fill with this sacred smoke. When proposing to work important rituals of protection and exorcism, burn other resins, such as frankincense or copal together, at the same time, actively believing and visually seeing the negativity departing as the smoke engulfs the area. Let this burn down until the resins turn to a dark paste; then place a few more nuggets on that to repeat the process, remembering to keep on envisioning the bad being transformed to good—the bad wafting away to the heavens to be recycled. Know in your heart that all you have done has been completed. Know that your ritual has worked.

Theban Negativity Releasing Ritual

For this spell, you will need:

1. A large metal bowl or cauldron

2. Two or three ignitable charcoal bricks

3. A quill and black ink

4. Parchment paper

5. Two black and white candles; straight or votive will do nicely.

Here is an ancient method for the release and banishment of all things akin to negativity. The most likely method to be evident in almost all cultures and religious sects, whether it is called a "fire ritual" or "the wafting of sacred smoke," this method is believed to be a direct link to the heavens.

Although seemingly mystical at first glance, it has found its way into the therapeutic setting. Because this ritual allows a person to let go of old business and pent-up pain, one can see the benefits. As the anger, sadness, and grief may be seen as reality in our society, it's understandable why so many today simply cannot find release or closure. Here, however, the ritual is designed specifically to set such emotional weight and stress free, literally burning it away, to become nothing more than smoke that will dissolve away.

Here's what you do: During the waning moon, take your pot or cauldron and set it in your backyard or sacred outdoor space.

While facing true north, light the charcoal blocks in the cauldron and wait until they are red hot. Place one black candle to the left of you (you may wish to surround the candles with an open top glass tube to keep wind at bay) and the white candle to your right. Now you will light the black candle first, then the white candle. As the black candle will draw in existing negative energies, and the white candle purifies the area from where this ritual takes place, this location becomes both grounded and sacred.

After this is done, sit on the earth and be as still as you can. This is your opportunity to become centered and focused on your problems, situations, or any issue you want resolved. Sit and contemplate. Visualize every detail of your problems; the same problems or issue that you have been sustaining, actually feeding with your energy and soul over the years. Once you have accounted for all the damage that these issues have been causing over the many years, itemizing every one in your mind, you will now transfer these poison-filled hardships and, with quill and ink, write them on your parchment paper. Be sure to apply each and every item to the paper, leaving nothing out.

Once that is complete, roll up the parchment tightly and hold it in both your hands. With eyes shut and mind only on the issues at hand, visualize the paper catching fire, filling the air with smoke, and then disappearing altogether. Listen for the tiny screams of these little daemons, screaming to be freed. As this is taking place, give this scroll of pain and grief over to the fire. As you make sure the parchment is completely burning away, take your hands and form two separate cups. Now, waft the smoke upward to the heavens and say aloud your intent for never having those old habits, painful memories, or old emotional wounds ever return.

When you are finished and the paper is reduced to ash, snuff out the black candle, and then the white. Turn the cauldron upside down, and give thanks to the heavens for taking in the discarded filth of your mortal life. You may also wish to place offerings of sweet herbs and milk outside where the parchment and charcoal ashes lie. This is believed to serve as thanks to the elemental spirits.

THEBAN HOME CLEANSING RITUAL

For this spell you will need:

1. One bundle of dried Mediterranean, Mexican, or standard European sage.

2. One cup of sea salt or kosher salt.

3. Two feet of black yarn.

4. A large sea shell or metal dish.

5. Four pieces of parchment paper and a pen.

6. Four garden variety rocks or stones.

7. A natural straw broom.

This is one of my favorite cleansing rituals, and is believed to date back to Medieval times, but may in fact be much older. The use of sage, although used primarily by Native Americans as a negativity banishing herb, as well as for the instilling of wisdom and visions, has seen similar magickal uses by many of the spiritual mindset.

In this ritual, sage (*Salvia officinalis* or *Salvia apiana*) is used primarily for disbanding negative build-up and for the exorcizing of the home; however, it will also aid in issues of clairvoyance, consecration, divination, healing, inspiration, longevity, love, peace, prosperity, protection, psychic awareness, and obtaining wisdom. When smoldered slowly, the magickal attributes find a way throughout your home or sacred space, literally chasing away the negative characteristics of misfortune and evil. This herb also grounds and sanctifies.

Sea salt or kosher salt, when sprinkled around your home, acts as a barrier that will keep negative influences from entering your home, as well as psychically repelling people of a dark or evil nature. The broom is used in the spiritual and magickal realm in very much the same fashion, for sweeping out the negative aspects of our complicated world.

First, take a few moments and write on each of the separate pieces of parchment paper an individual Theban letter, which will act as psychic barriers. The letters might be arranged as follows:

1. ⁊, which stands for *rage* and *negative temperament*

2. ᙢ, which stands for *emotional interference* and *psychic disturbance*

3. 🜚, which stands for *tranquility* and *joy*

4. 🜚, which stands for *protection* and *security*

Once this is done, go to each of the four main corners of your home, beginning with the northernmost corner. If there is a corner for each of the four earthly directions, that's great. If not, however, go to the corner that is closest to North, and place the parchment with the Theban letter *M* on the floor, up tight to the two connecting walls. In clockwise fashion, go the corner nearest to the East and do the same with the Theban letter *R*. Follow the clockwise pattern to the South corner with the Theban letter *T*, and finally to the West corner with the Theban letter *Y*. After each piece of parchment has been placed in its designated corner, place a rock or stone on each of the papers, in the same aforementioned clockwise fashion.

Once this is complete, take the sea salt or kosher salt and stand at the main doorway, just outside of your home. Beginning at the righthand side, walk around your home pouring the salt close to the walls as you walk around your entire structure. If you live in an apartment or dormitory, you may do this from within that structure in the same fashion. As you reach the doorway from where you started, stop and return inside your home and shut the door.

Now you will begin the ever-popular ritual of sage burning. To do this, simply wrap the sage leaves together with the black yarn, or you may use store-bought sage sticks, found at most New Age stores, and light it on one end. Hold it over your sea shell or metal dish and follow throughout your entire home, starting at the North corner, and following to the East, then the South, and finally the West corner. There's no hurry, as your sage stick will smolder for some time. When you're done with this, simply lay the sage stick in the sea shell or the dish and stand at the center of your home. Take a few moments and visualize all the negativity and psychic filth lying all over the floor before you. Now you're ready for the final part of the cleansing.

When you're ready, open the front door and retrieve your straw broom. As with everyday sweeping, vigorously and purposely begin sweeping the negativity and psychic filth out the main doorway, saying aloud that you will not tolerate such rubbish and muck staying in your home. Conduct this ritual until you feel satisfied about your cleaning job, knowing that you have cleaned your home with passion, will, and intention.

Once this is complete, take the remainder of your sea salt and pour it around the doorway from outside. Connect the salt from one end to the other, and then shut the door. Your home is clean. Keep the parchment papers and the rocks, securing them in place until the following morning. At exactly the same time as you began this ritual the day before, collect the parchment papers from North to West in a clockwise fashion and take them outside. In a small hole beyond your property, bury these papers and the remains of the sage stick. You would do this as if it were a dead and diseased thing. Brush off your hands when done and say the following: *Now you are dead and done; no more shall you make my life undone. Your stench of evil and scent of wrong will no longer reek in my home or lungs, for no more will your presence be known to me or those I love. It is done!*

THEBAN INCENSE MONEY RITUAL

For this spell you will need:

1. A brass, copper, silver, or steel bowl.

2. One or two tablespoons of powdered clove, which can be purchased at most grocery stores.

3. A sheet of parchment paper or natural undyed cotton.

4. Black Magic Marker.

5. One green candle. Small votives will do nicely.

As with the aforementioned ritual, the basic tools needed are the same. The difference, however, is in the herb and the color of the candle used. The context in which the Theban script is used is the representation of prosperity. The sacred herb is the aromatic clove (*Syzygium aromatic*). Clove is used in ritual magick as a drawing agent for purification and love, but is also burned as an addendum for many prosperity rituals.

For the spell of increasing wealth, take the pure powder of clove, which may be purchased at your local supermarket or grocer, and place a small amount in a metal censer or bowl. Light the top of the powder and let it smolder. While the incense is burning, filling the air with its mysterious scent, light the green candle and place it behind the bowl. As the powder will burn down naturally, this is the time to write your desires on the parchment, remembering that you should ask only for that which is needed and not be greedy. Use the corresponding Theban letters to enforce and empower your goals.

As the smoke from the smoldering powder lifts up into the air, envision yourself surrounded by money. Gold coins, silver coins, copper coins, there is an abundance flowing around you. See the floor from where you sit or stand covered with the green leaves of wealth, getting deeper and deeper. Know that your desires will be answered and that all you need will come to be. You may also burn clove when you wish to clear the air of stress and sadness, as this is a sacred scent that will whisk you off to enlightened states of mind and soul.

Theban Candle Magick

The subject of candle magick is almost as old as humanity itself, as certainly early humans were able to look at the natural reality of the flame in a far more elemental manner than do their modern counterparts. Yet, even after thousands of years—long past the empires of ancient Egypt, Babylon, and Rome; beyond the sacred temples of Delphi, Apollo, or Atlantis—the enigma of the flame continues to awe and inspire modern practitioners of the old religion.

In this section, I have included a brief listing of common candle magick information, which is built largely on European, Asian, and Native American sources. Because it would go beyond the scope of this book's intent to cover the immense realities of candle magick and its significance to spell casting and ritual, I am only offering the very basics here, but invite you to research more deeply this rather large subject, understanding that the methods and philosophies of candle magick within the Theban perspective are as large and as beneficial as your imagination.

The following list of basic candle colors may certainly be used within the scheme of Theban magick; however, it is my fervent belief that personal choice and psychic impression are as vital and as accepted as any traditional form of magick, meaning that you may pick and choose personal power colors or colors that best fit your psychic need, in juxtaposition to your Zodiac colors. For instance, my Zodiac colors (I'm a Cancer) are white, pale blue, and silver. My personal power colors are forest green, black, and Indigo. Therefore, I may wish to use these colors along with my Zodiac colors to boost the power of my intended goals of magick.

BASIC CANDLE COLORS

White and corresponding colors silver, metallic blue, and pale gray represent peace, purity, spirituality, enlightenment, cleansing, clairvoyance, healing, and truth seeking. Rituals involving moon magick and purification prefer white as the primary source color. White candles are specifically burned during cleansing and protection rituals.

Black and corresponding color dark gray are used primarily for the banishment of negativity. With its negativity absorbing powers, this color, or more appropriately, this regulatory color, also aids in transition rituals from the old into the new. Because black, in truth, lacks "color," it is seen as a drawing agent, which sucks in negative aspects, then burns the remains to smoke. Use this candle to banish evil and negativity, as well as for uncrossing and hex-breaking rituals. Use black for casting out all negative energies, and for absorbing illnesses and bad habits.

Red and corresponding colors dark red, maroon, scarlet, and crimson are powerful and active colors, which symbolize vitality, health, energy, strength, sexual prowess, and courage. Use these colors of candles for health, body, and strength rituals, as well as for obtaining and maintaining physical energy, passion, and sexual powers within protection magick. Because red is the color of fire, you should use this color with respect to heat and power issues. It is associated with life and death, strength, and raw power.

Yellow and corresponding colors bright or light yellow and mustard are colors of mental prowess and intellect. Yellow serves the command of memory, creative imagination, communication, and mental alertness. Employ this color to entice and aid in activity, creativity, concentration, and imagination rituals. Burn yellow candles to increase visualization techniques and for personal power when studying and researching. Because yellow is representative of the solar cycle, burn such a candle to stimulate your mind and consciousness.

Green and corresponding colors light green, apple green, and olive are the quintessential colors of money, wealth, and health-related rituals. These colors stands for abundance, fertility, good luck, and harmony, as well as money, prosperity, employment, fertility, healing, growth, and abundance. Green is an elemental color, the color of the earth and the living growth upon it. Burn a green candle for money and prosperity rituals when seeking new employment or when needing a raise.

Blue and corresponding colors light blue, sky blue, and pale pink are the colors of healing, truth, inspiration, higher wisdom, occult power, psychic protection, and deep understanding. Use blue for rituals involving healing, peaceful feelings, patience, and happiness. Combine blue with purple to evoke psychic awareness or when having problems sleeping, through visualization magick.

Orange and corresponding colors light orange, gold, and bronze represent attraction, energy, and the increase of physical energies. Burn orange to attract specific physical goals during meditation and visualization rituals. When combined with gold and bronze colored candles, visualize the cosmos blessing you with money, fortune, and good luck.

Purple and corresponding colors light purple and royal blue are suited for issues of power, success, and psychic manifestation. Use them for finding spiritual and psychic independence, for financial gain, and to contact, invoke, or evoke the higher levels of consciousness and psychic awareness.

Gray and corresponding colors silver gray, burnt red, and brown work well for protection magick and spell crafting as well as issues involving animals. Considered to be neutral colors, they're used when in deep contemplation of complex issues. These colors work well with meditation, as they neutralize many negative influences.

Silver and gold, and corresponding colors white or any metallic, and base colors in combined sequential patterns that form a rainbow, represent the higher levels of clairvoyance, astral energies, channeling, and memories of past lives. Silver, much like black, will aid in removing negativity, at the same time encouraging patience and stability. It also aids in developing psychic abilities and intuition.

Blue-green and corresponding colors indigo blue, pale green, and sea green are considered royal and high-achieving colors. Use these colors for finding peaceful resolutions to personal problems, especially during positive visualization and mediation rituals.

Magenta and corresponding colors blood red, reddish yellow, and any vibrant combination of red and violet aid in the banishment of harmful intent from outside forces. Use magenta for fast modifications and luck rituals, as well as for spiritual healing and rites of exorcism.

CANDLE PREPARATION AND ANOINTING

When preparing for ritual in candle magick, it is important to understand that there are many diverse methods to follow, and by no means is it necessary to choose one method alone. It is necessary, however, to have complete faith and belief in your intended goal of magick before anything will happen, as without belief there is no reason in the ritual.

One method I use is anointing the candles in order to empower them with a specific authority and intent. For instance, I may anoint my candle by rubbing a specific oil: a power oil such as a Zodiac oil. I might also wish to use an essential oil that corresponds to my intended goal. If my ritual were based on the acquisition of wealth and prosperity, I would use green, silver, and gold candles and *anoint* them with patchouli oil. Although there are likely to be countless techniques and magick methods in doing this, you may choose what works best for you.

When anointing a straight candle, which is *consecrating*, hold the candle in the center, and from the center, rub the oil outward to the base, then again to the wick. When using an enclosed candle such as those in a glass, simply rub the oil over its surface and wick, and then let it dry naturally. Additionally, you may wish to perform a simple verbal blessing over the candles in order to spiritually empower them, as well as carve the Theban letter to aid in your magickal ritual.

CARVING THEBAN SYMBOLS

Since the invention of candles, people have carved various symbols on them in order to empower and consecrate by magickal means. Whether carved with astrological, runic, alchemical, or numerical symbols, the general purpose is to ensure that your magick intent is modified and strengthened. To this end, the Theban example, in the context of candle magick, will act accordingly.

Because such carvings are designed to signify and justify each individual desire, as well as to help in the organization of the candles when there are many during ritual, the reasoning becomes clear. As each Theban letter houses a very specific meaning, one must truly think about those meanings in relation to his desire or situation. Remember: belief, patience, and tenacity are the only ways to open spiritual doors for you. The only substance that remains is the ability to see your works of magick come to fruition. When you apply ritual candle magick during the divination process, don't be surprised if you see a direct correlation to your issues or problems within the revelation. Indeed, it is plain to see that magick is truly alive and well in the Theban Oracle!

Chapter Seven

CONSTRUCTING AND CARING FOR YOUR THEBAN STONES

N ow that you have a good grasp of the ancient art of divination and its true uses, it's time to consider what tool you
wish to make, as the choices are vast and fairly personal. In ancient
times it was common to use items of the earth to construct such
tools of divination. Many Asian cultures used pieces of shell or
bone in the art of *ji g* divination, and live crustaceans in a practice
known as *nggàm*. The ancient Greeks would have used the entrails
of animals, while the Vikings might have used sea shells and animal bones to foretell the outcome of battles and journeys, centuries before the 17th-century version of the rune stone was created.
Indeed, there are hundreds of methods the ancients used to tell
their futures. Although the popular tools are mostly made of paper,
as in the Tarot card, or a synthetic clay, as with many rune stone kits
on the market today, the best and truest are those articles made of
the earth, which harm no living creatures in the process.

In order to follow this edict, I have a simple method that is as ancient as those used by the Celts and Vikings and as commonplace as the high temples of antediluvian magick in early Christian Europe. The true tools of divination were and remain simple articles of nature that hold their own "power," which absorbs and retains various energies from the user and nature alike. Because the ancients believed in such things, their tools would have been made from simple articles, cared for and guarded with great regard. Of the tools used, stones, sea shells, bone, and wood were the most common in the ancient world, being made by the practitioner and routinely cleaned and then stored in a sacred place until further use. Wishing to remain true to the ancient methods, I feel these articles are indeed the best, and relatively easy to acquire and make.

One of the best materials is the simple polished pebble, which can be bought in many crafting stores and can be found in various sizes, though no more than three inches in diameter. These stones are inexpensive and come in interesting colors, like reds, yellows, greens, and shades of white. They are good to paint the Theban letters on or to etch them with an engraving tool. There are other artifacts from nature that work well too, like wood chips or animal bones, and both can be made using the same method as the pebbles. Either way, you won't have to put much effort into making your Theban stones or bones; you'll just need to choose your particular path.

If deciding on wood chips, like the popular *Ogham staves* of Celtic tradition, simply purchase or whittle two- to three-inch disks

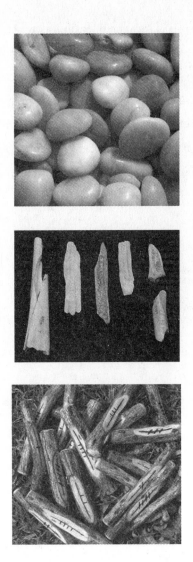

Pebbles, animal bone, and wood staves can all be used
for carving or painting the Theban letters

and paint or etch the Theban letters on them. Or use bleached and dried chicken bones or common sea shells to re-create a process like that of the Zulu Sangoma diviners of South Africa. Whatever method you pick, however, you'll find that making your own tools of divination is not only enjoyable but profoundly personal, creating a bond between practitioner and the article of nature one chooses. It will be your soulful expression that makes your process the most powerful.

Protection and Cleansing Techniques

Historically, within the realms of both low and high magick, there are various rules and methodologies to follow. Be it for the preparation of magickal workings, or when following the various techniques involved, select rules and regulations are as important as your belief in the mystical arts. From the sacred place in which to practice and meditate, to looking after the tools of ritual, the methodologies that accompany each and every aspect of such workings are vital to your overall dealings in magick arts. Whether involved in the preparation of herbal concoctions and remedies, or when partaking in the ritual of meditation or prayer, it is imperative to tend to the many rules and edicts that apply.

Though there may be many methods to adhere to, remember that these precautions are designed to make sure you are protecting both yourself and your tools from harmful negativities that are always waiting to show up and dismantle all that you have done. Here too, such rules of protection should apply to your Theban tools, whether stone, wood, sea shell, or bone. Without a doubt, the common practice of protection has many separate, as well as similar techniques to follow. When soothsayers used the crystal, or black mirror for scrying, for instance, it was common to wrap such tools in a natural black cloth for the express purpose of protecting them from negative influences from all planes of existence. Your Theban tools should require the same practice, if not encased in a dark-colored carrying bag. Because the black cloth is believed to repel the negative drawing powers that coexist along with the positive, it's a good idea to apply this method to your personal articles too.

To further your protection cycle, I suggest the rudimentary practice of cleansing your Theban tools. There are two distinct methods of doing this. The first method is to gently wash and rinse your tools in simple salt water. If you do not live near an ocean, simply purchase a small bag of sea salt. You can find genuine sea salt in most grocery stores and health food markets, but to have the highest quality of sea salt, I suggest you find a source that sells Dead Sea salt from Israel, as this and most store-bought kosher sea salts are considered the most pure, especially within ritual.

Once you have your sea salt, simply apply natural spring water to a bowl or chalice, and stir in a tablespoon or two of the salt with your finger. When the salt and water are well mixed, gently wash your stones, shells, or bones completely and set them on a plate to dry. When you're finished, simply wipe them with a clean cloth and place in the accompanying bag until your next gaming process. For wood chips, gently rub the dry sea salts over each, lovingly caressing each wooden disk while envisioning a white light going into it and dark, negative energies flowing out.

Although this is the most uncomplicated method to use, you may wish to add several tablespoons of dried mugwort and hyssop herbs to the salt mixture. This is said to be a powerful protection additive that will not only reverse negative influences that may attach to your tools over time, but will also serve as an invisible shield against further negative influences for future use. If other people may be using your tools, leaving their own vibrations, be they good or ill, the stones will draw in each and every particle of the psychic residue that we all leave behind. Therefore, it is a wise practice to clean your Theban tools and all tools of ritual whenever they are being handled by others.

When using this cleansing method for tools made of metal, such as the athame, chalices, bells, or talismans, remember that the salt will act as a corrosive; therefore you will need to take further measures in order to retard this damaging effect. I find that natural oils such as grapeseed, hazelnut, and olive oil make wonderful protecting barriers, as well as excellent carriers for magickal herbs. One or more of these oils mixed with a good amount of the dried mugwort and hyssop, for instance, makes a worthy protection oil. After agitating the herbs with the oil, the magickal qualities are transferred throughout. For a final step in protection from negativity, you may wish to place your Theban tools within a natural wooden box for safekeeping. Add to that a few smoky quartz crystals and pieces of the ancient petrified wood known as jet to help absorb any remaining negativity. This time-honored process has been used by the wise for centuries, believed to act as a repulsive shield against ill will and negative magick sent by others. Remember, just as we keep our bodies clean, thus taking the necessary precautions against getting sick, the same is true for your Theban divination process as well.

THEBAN ASSOCIATION CHART

During the Middle Ages, when great oppression and strife had filled the lands, and when the holy inquisitions condemned and murdered all whom they believed evil, wizard and magi, cunning men and women, and the assemblers of high magick had banded together to save the written works of the ancients from the flames of intolerance and hatred. Eight hundred and eleven of Europe's elite magi from both near and far had gathered together to save the sacred writings, manuscripts, and ancient tomes of wisdom. An enigmatic occult scholar known as Honorius of Thebes, the son of Euclid and the Master of the Thebans, was assigned the mission of collecting said works of magick, and then condensing the ancient works into seven sacred tomes, each to contain ninety-three chapters. With this, one of the greatest mysteries of history was born. Within these sacred tomes the Theban alphabet was created to serve as a secret cipher to translate the works of magick and ritual ceremony into the arcane, in order to baffle the witch-hunter generals and evil clergymen. Although many of those articles of Medieval and Renaissance magick were to remain a conundrum of history, the beautiful Theban alphabet had so been assigned the role of mystery.

Below are the Theban letters, their Latin and Hebrew equivalents, the historical luminaries that they represent, the corresponding function of magick and divination, their sacred herbs, and the divine angelic order they represent.

ꓦ, A, AIEPH: *Joan of Arc*
Divinatory Meaning: *The journey ahead, change, a new development*
Sacred Herb: *Lavender*
Angelic Order: *Thrones*

ꓩ, B, BETH: *King Solomon*
Divinatory Meaning: *Intellect, pride, divine wisdom, abundance*
Sacred Herb: *Hyssop*
Angelic Order: *Seraphim*

ꟿ, C, GIMEL: *Zoroaster*
Divinatory Meaning: *An inner power, self-realization, divine
    understanding*
Sacred Herb: *Sweet orange*
Angelic Order: *Dominions*

ꟽ, D, DALETH: *Nostradamus*
Divinatory Meaning: *Self-restraint, reflection, flow, transformation*

Sacred Herb: *Rose*
Angelic Order: *Virtues*

ꝺ, E, HAI: *Petrus de Abano*
Divinatory Meaning: *Friendship, distinguished companionship,*
 partnership
Sacred Herb: *Myrrh*
Angelic Order: *Archangels*

ꝩ, F, WAW: *Johannes Faustus*
Divinatory Meaning: *A warning, fear, ignorance, self-loathing*
Sacred Herb: *Mugwort*
Angelic Order: *Angels*

�, G, ZAIN: *Hypatia of Alexandria*
Divinatory Meaning: *The sovereign feminine spirit, inward wisdom,*
 the pursuit of enlightenment
Sacred Herb: *Sandalwood*
Angelic Order: *Dominions*

ꝩ, H, CHETH: *Dr. John Dee*
Divinatory Meaning: *Concentration, thought, wise decisions*
Sacred Herb: *Carnation*
Angelic Order: *Cherubim*

Ʋ, I/J, TETH: *Abu-Ma'shar*
Divinatory Meaning: *Life cycle, natural order, cosmic upheaval*
Sacred Herb: *Rosemary*
Angelic Order: *Seraphim*

ꂕ, K, YOD: *Johannes Trithemius*
Divinatory Meaning: *Discipline, regulation, self-order, divine
     nourishment*
Sacred Herb: *Jasmine*
Angelic Order: *Powers*

Ɀ, L, KAAW: *Dr. Simon Forman*
Divinatory Meaning: *Stagnation, languishing, persecution, surrender*
Sacred Herb: *Garlic*
Angelic Order: *Thrones*

ꝛ, M, LAMES: *Gilles de Rais*
Divinatory Meaning: *Rage, negative temperament, ending of innocence*
Sacred Herb: *Stinging nettle*
Angelic Order: *Virtues*

ꝳ, N, MEM: *Dr. Nicholas Flamel*
Divinatory Meaning: *Willpower, a crusade, a priceless gift*
Sacred Herb: *Frankincense*
Angelic Order: *Cherubim*

♏, O, MM: *William Lilly*
Divinatory Meaning: *Divine understanding, angelic overseeing, transitional harmony*
Sacred Herb: *Myrtle*
Angelic Order: *Principalities*

♍, P, SAMECH: *Paracelsus*
Divinatory Meaning: *A sacrifice, solitude, the sacred quest*
Sacred Herb: *Clove*
Angelic Order: *Virtues*

♃, Q, AIM: *Cornelius Agrippa*
Divinatory Meaning: *Endurance, steadfastness, rectification, balance*
Sacred Herb: *Fennel seed*
Angelic Order: *Virtues*

♏, R, PEI: *Robert Fludd*
Divinatory Meaning: *Interference, disturbance, submission, withdrawal*
Sacred Herb: *Camphor*
Angelic Order: *Dominions*

♉, S, TZADDI: *Giordano Bruno*
Divinatory Meaning: *Wealth, a tribute, a spiritual path, the unseen*
Sacred Herb: *Mint*
Angelic Order: *Seraphim*

ꝯ, T, QOPH: *Lao Tzu*
Divinatory Meaning: *Tranquility, simplicity, joy*
Sacred Herb: *Benzoin*
Angelic Order: *Cherubim*

ꝼ, U/V/W, REISCH: *Imhotep*
Divinatory Meaning: *The true male significance, divine silence, emotional transition*
Sacred Herb: *Cedar wood*
Angelic Order: *Principalities*

ꝶ, X, SHEIN: *Honorius of Thebes*
Divinatory Meaning: *Darkness and light, coexisting differences, misconception, judgment*
Sacred Herb: *Juniper*
Angelic Order: *Archangels*

ꝷ, Y, TAW: *Albertus Magnus*
Divinatory Meaning: *Cherubic protection, security, divine mortality*
Sacred Herb: *Mistletoe*
Angelic Order: *Archangels*

ꝸ, Z, ZED: *Merlin*
Divinatory Meaning: *A portal or entrance, an elevated transposition*
Sacred Herb: *Pine*
Angelic Order: *Seraphim*

♃ Ending Stone: *Of unknown origin*

Divinatory Meaning: *Ending to a life process, life transition,*
  juxtaposition

Sacred Herb: *Sage*

Angelic Order: *Powers*

Mystery Stone: *Bethany*

Divinatory Meaning: *An unknowable path, the mystery of arcane*
  origins, spiritual freedom

Sacred Herb: *unknown*

Angelic Order: *unknown*

BIBLIOGRAPHY

Agrippa, Heinrich Cornelius. *Three Books of Occult Philosophy.* Translated by James French. (London: 1651).

Agrippa, Heinrich Cornelius. *Three Books of Occult Philosophy* (Antwerp: 1539); edited and translated by Donald Tyson (Woodbury, MN: Llewellyn Publications, 2004).

Barrett, Francis. *The Magus* (London: Lackington, Allen, and Co., Temple of the Muses, 1801).

Barrett, David V. *The New Believers: A Survey of Sects, Cults and Alternative Religions* (London: Cassell & Co., 2001).

Bias, Clifford. *Ritual Book of Magic* (York Beach, ME: Weiser, 1981).

Butler, E. M. *Ritual Magic* (Cambridge: Cambridge University Press, 1949).

Burnham, Sophy. *A Book of Angels* (New York: Ballantine Books, 1990).

Cunningham, Scott. *Cunningham's Encyclopedia of Magical Herbs* (Woodbury, MN: Llewellyn Publications, 1993).

Davis, R. T. *Four Centuries of Witch Beliefs* (London: Methuen, 1947).

Davidson, Gustav. *A Dictionary of Angels* (New York: The Free Press, 1994).

Frazer, Sir James George. *The Golden Bough: A Study in Magic and Religion* (New York: Simon & Schuster, 1922).

Gaebelein, A. C. *What the Bible Says About Angels* (Grand Rapids, MI: Baker Book House, 1987).

Gettings, Fred. *Dictionary of Occult, Hermetic Alchemical Sigils* (London: Routledge & Kegan Paul, 1981).

Godwin, Malcolm. *Angels.* (New York: Simon & Schuster, 1990).

Graham, Billy. *Angels* (Dallas: Word Publishing, 1986).

Grimble, Arthur. *Return to the Islands* (London: John Murray, 1957).

Guiley, Rosemary Ellen. *Angels* (New York: Checkmark Books, 2004).

Guiley, Rosemary Ellen. *The Encyclopedia of Witches and Witchcraft*, 2nd Ed. (New York: Facts On File, 1999).

Hedegård, Gösta. *Liber Iuratus Honorii: A Critical Edition of the Latin Version of the Sworn Book of Honorius* (Stockholm: Almovist & Wiksell International, 2002).

King, Francis X. *Witchcraft and Demonology* (New York: Hamlyn Publishing Group, 1987).

Kirby, W. F. *Kalevala* (London: J. M. Dent, 1907).

Leavell, Landrum P. *Angels, Angels, Angels* (Nashville: Broadman Press, 1973).

Lewis, James, and Evelyn Oliver. *Angels A to Z* (Detroit: Visible Ink Press, 1996).

Luk, A. D. K. *The Law of Life: Book II.* (Pueblo, CO: A. D. K. Luk Publications, 1989).

Masello, Robert. *Fallen Angels* (New York: Berkley Publishing Group, 1994).

Morgan, Lawrence. *Flute of the Sand* (London: Odhams Press, 1956).

Paracelsus. *The Architoxes of Magic.* Translated by Robert Turner (London: 1656).

Prophet, Elizabeth Clare. *How to Work With Angels* (Livingston, MT: Summit University Press, 1996).

Prophet, Elizabeth Clare and Mark L. Prophet. *Saint Germain on Alchemy: For the Adept in the Aquarian Age* (Livingston, MT: Summit University Press, 1986).

Thorndike, Lynn. *History of Magic and Experimental Science,* Vols. 5 and 6, *Sixteenth Century* (New York: Columbia University Press, 1941).

Thompson, R. C. *Semitic Magic* (London: Luzac & Co., 1908).

Trachtenberg, J. *Semitic Magic and Superstition* (New York: Behrman House, 1939).

Waite, Arthur Edward. *The Book of Ceremonial Magic* (New York: Bell Publishing, 1889).

Whitcomb, Bill. *The Magician's Companion: A Practical and Encyclopedic Guide to Magical and Religious Symbolism* (Woodbury, MN: Llewellyn Publications, 1993).

Zolar. *Zolar's Encyclopedia of Ancient and Forbidden Knowledge* (New York: Prentice Hall, 1970).

Manuscripts

Magical Treatises by Caius, Simon Forman, John Dee, and Edward Kelly; British Museum, Add. MS. 36,674, 16th century.

Tractacus Magici et Astrologici, British Museum, Sloane MS. 3821.

Schema Magicum, British Museum, Sloane MS. 430, 14th century.

De Maleficiis, British Museum, Sloane MS. 3529, 16th century.

Liber Iuratus Honorii: The Sworne Booke of Honoryus: A Translation of a Book of Magic. British Museum, Sloane MS. 3854, 15th century.

Web Page References

Copeland, Mark. "Ministering Spirits: Angels in the Old Testament." *www.ccel.org.*

Copeland, Mark. "Terms and Descriptions of Angels." *www.ccel.org.*

Fares, Aymen. "Angelics and the Angelic Realm." *www.spiritual.com.*

Tatum, Johnny. "The Hierarchy of Angels: Hierarchical Chart of Angels." *http://radicalgrace.com.*

Tatum, Johnny. "The Hierarchy of Angels: Distinguishing the Higher Ranked." *http://radicalgrace.com.*

The Bible searchable online version. *https://www.bible.com/bible/*

ABOUT THE AUTHOR

Greg Jenkins, Ph.D. (Th.D.), M.Sc., has worked for more than twenty years in the mental health and medical fields and is currently a mental health professional, case manager, and pastoral counselor. Greg is the founder and director of Soulful Expressions: Independent Art Survey and Psychological Consulting, an organization that conducts research into the meanings of patient artwork and other hands-on creations, as well as facilitating therapeutic groups and seminars. Greg is an avid folklorist and collector of urban legends, as well as an acquirer of many artifacts pertaining to the occult and preternatural. Greg is an associate member of England's Society for Psychical Research, is a member of the Parapsychological Association, and is creator of the International Consortium for Psychical Research and Paranormal Inquiry. He is the author of *Florida's Ghostly Legends and Haunted Folklore, Volumes 1–3; Chronicles of the Strange and Uncanny in Florida;* and the *St. Augustine Guide to Haunted Bed and Breakfast Inns, Pubs and Eateries.* Also due this year: *Renaissance Cooking in Today's Kitchen: Magical Feasts of the Paganus Folk.* This book is published by Schiffer Publishing and will be out mid-2014.

TO OUR READERS